Sun Dogs
and
Shooting Stars

Sun Dogs
and
Shooting Stars

A SKYWATCHER'S CALENDAR

By Franklyn M. Branley

Illustrated by True Kelley

HOUGHTON MIFFLIN COMPANY BOSTON

Library of Congress Cataloging in Publication Data

Branley, Franklyn Mansfield, 1915-
  Sun dogs and shooting stars.

  Bibliography: p.
  SUMMARY: A guide to astronomical and meteorologi-
cal events typical of each month, from the beginning
of winter through summer's meteor showers and
hail to the harvest moon of autumn.
    1. Astronomy — Observers' manuals — Juvenile litera-
ture. 2. Meteorology — Observers' manuals —
Juvenile literature.   [1. Astronomy — Observers'
manuals. 2. Meteorology — Observers' manuals]
I. Kelley, True.   II. Title.
QB63.B82   523   80-17430
ISBN 0-395-29520-3

Printed in the United States of America

V 10 9 8 7 6 5 4 3 2

To Roma Gans

CONTENTS

The Autumn Stars   87

The Calendar

You don't have to be a skilled skywatcher to know that time is going by. As a day passes, the sun rises and sets, shadows grow short with the approach of noon and lengthen at sunset. As a year passes, the long shadows of winter become the shorter shadows of summer. Seasons change from winter snow and ice to the warm, balmy days of July and August.

Such changes made it possible for primitive people to reckon time. An event might have occurred so many harvests ago, or so many sunrises—or full moons, for that matter.

As people developed societies, and began to trade back and forth, more precise ways of keeping track of time were needed. And so various people—the Babylonians, Chinese, Hebrews, Mayas, Aztecs, Hindus, Greeks, and Romans—developed calendars. Our calendar is based upon the Roman calendar that was introduced by Julius Caesar in 46 B.C. and which, in turn, was based upon the calendar of the Egyptians.

1

The word *calendar* comes from the Roman word *kalends* (or "callings"), the first day of each month in the early Roman year. In Roman times a month began when the crescent moon appeared. Priests watched the skies, and as soon as this sliver of a moon was seen, they called out the news. *Calendar* now refers to the entire modern system of reckoning days, months, and years.

The basic natural clock of time keeping is the earth. A day is the time it takes for the earth to complete one rotation on its axis. In a rough way the interval can be measured simply by changes in shadows. If you measure the shadow of a stick, you'll find that it is very long in the morning. At noon the shadow is shortest, and as sunset approaches, the shadow lengthens. A day is the interval between appearances of the noontime shadow.

ONE DAY
23 hours · 56 minutes 4.09 seconds

A day is a "natural" time interval. So are a month and a year. As we use it today, the month is based on the revolution of the moon around the earth. But as

2

you know, months are of different lengths — 31 days, 30 days, and 28 (or 29 in leap years) — so the connection with the period of revolution must be only approximate. (The time required for the moon to go around the earth is closer to 27⅓ days.) The relation of months and days would be greatly simplified if there were an even number of days in a month.

The same sort of problem exists between days and years. A year is the time required for Earth to go once around the sun. During the interval, it would be fine if the earth rotated an even number of times. But it doesn't. In one year the earth rotates 365¼ times. Historically, that quarter day led to great confusion.

ONE YEAR
365 days · 6 hours
9 minutes · 9 seconds

A calendar is a man-made device that attempts to adjust natural events such as seasonal changes to dates of the year. If no adjustments were made, that quarter day would become a day in 4 years, 10 days in 40 years, 100 days in 400 years. The seasons and the calendar would be out of step — we'd have summer weather in December and winter weather in July.

To avoid such confusion, Julius Caesar introduced leap years. And in 1582 Pope Gregory improved the idea. To keep the seasons in step with the calendar, a day is added to February every 4 years—in those years divisible by 4. The last year of every century is also a leap year, but only when the number of the century is divisible by 400. The year 2000 will be a leap year; the year 2100 will not. That would seem to take care of the problem, but it doesn't. After a long while an extra day has to be eliminated, so every century divisible by 4000 is not a leap year. The year 4000 and multiples of it—8000, 12,000, 16,000— will not be leap years. By making all these adjustments the calendar will be kept in step with the seasons (or the sun's position) for some 20,000 years.

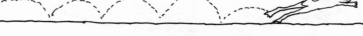

Incidentally, February 29 is called leap day because after that day, the days will "leap" over. If in a given year March 3 is a Tuesday, let us say, it will be a Wednesday the next year. But should the next year be a leap year, March 3 will be on Thursday: the calendar "leaps" one day.

Our calendar is the result of many efforts down through history, attempts to fit days into months evenly and months into years, although there is no even relation.

You may enjoy reading more about the calendar, so we've listed some books in the bibliography. This skywatchers' calendar is not just the calendar itself, but the sky and the changes that occur. We begin in the winter months, but you can start your skywatching at any time — spring, summer, or fall. All through the year, both night and day, there are things to observe in the sky above you. By watching and recording these sky events you can learn much about the changing year.

The Winter Stars

If you look southward about 9:00 P.M. toward the end of January you'll see Orion, a most impressive constellation containing bright stars. Around 9:00 P.M. in December, Orion will be about halfway east of south; in February it will be west of south. Orion is often called the winter constellation because it dominates the skies during the winter months.

The brightest star in Orion is Rigel. It is a blue-white, very brilliant, star that is actually 25,000 times brighter than the sun. Rigel appears less bright than the sun only because of its distance. It is about 900 light years away from the earth. The sun is thousands of times closer.

You may be able to see that Betelgeuse, the star in the upper-left section of Orion, is somewhat reddish. It is a red supergiant star that has a diameter some

500 times greater than the diameter of the sun, which is 1½ million kilometers.

Using the three stars of Orion's belt, Alnitak, Alnilam, and Mintaka, as guides, continue eastward and you'll see Sirius. Next to the sun, it is the brightest star in the sky. Its constellation is Canis Major, the Great Dog.

Following the same three stars and continuing westward, you come to Aldebaran, the brightest star in a "V" formation. The constellation is Taurus, the Bull.

8

Four dimmer stars just below Orion are in the constellation Lepus, the Hare.

Above Orion and a bit to the east are two bright stars, Castor and Pollux. They are in Gemini, the Twins.

Once you locate these stars, they will be easy to pick out. They will soon become familiar.

If you are not sure which direction is south, you can find it easily in the daytime before you start your starwatching. The noontime position of the sun is toward the south.

Before noon or after on a sunny day, you can use a watch to find south. You have to use a watch with hands, not a digital watch. Hold the watch flat and turn it so the hour hand points toward the sun. South is halfway between the hour hand and 12 on the dial.

DECEMBER

The early Romans had only 10 months in their calendar. The first month was March; the tenth was December; its name is from the Latin word *decem* ("ten").

In 46 B.C. Julius Caesar changed the calendar. Two new months, January and February, were put in front of March. This made December the twelfth month, in spite of its name.

The Anglo-Saxons, who lived in England a thousand years ago, called December *winter-monath,* or *heligh-monath* ("holy month") because Christmas comes in December.

In December the sun reaches its most southerly location, which signals the start of winter.

Measuring Sky Angles

Astronomers use angles to give the position of a star, or any other sky object. If a star is overhead they say its angle is 90 degrees; that means 90 degrees above the horizon. If it's halfway between the horizon and overhead it would be 45 degrees, a quarter of the way would be 22½ degrees, and so on.

Separation between stars is also given in angles. You imagine there is a line between you and one of the stars. This is the zero line. Then you imagine a line from you to the other star. The angle made by the two lines is the angle of separation between the two stars. For example, the "pointer" stars of the Big Dipper are separated by 5 degrees. The separation between Betelgeuse and Bellatrix in Orion is about 7 degrees.

While skywatching you can determine the angle of the moon, a star, or planet above the horizon, and you can measure the angle of separation of any two sky objects. Long ago astronomers made such measurements and they still do. Rough measurements can be made by "guessing." A quadrant will help you make more accurate measurements.

A quadrant includes 90 degrees, one fourth of a circle—*quad* means four. Elaborate quadrants were made in the sixteenth century by Tycho Brahe, a famous Danish astronomer, who was born December 14, 1546. The instruments were large, often twice as tall as a man. With these instruments Tycho was able to make accurate measurements of the positions and motions of the planets.

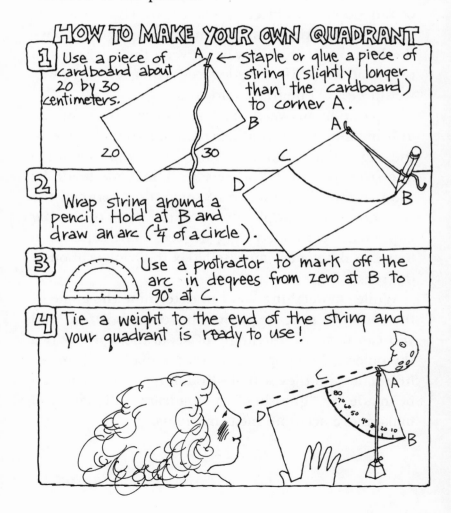

HOW TO MAKE YOUR OWN QUADRANT

1 Use a piece of cardboard about 20 by 30 centimeters.

← Staple or glue a piece of string (slightly longer than the cardboard) to corner A.

2 Wrap string around a pencil. Hold at B and draw an arc (¼ of a circle).

3 Use a protractor to mark off the arc in degrees from zero at B to 90° at C.

4 Tie a weight to the end of the string and your quadrant is ready to use!

You can make your own quadrant that will enable you to measure angles quite accurately. The main part is a piece of cardboard 20 by 30 centimeters, or thereabouts. The size is not critical. Staple or glue a piece of string to corner A of the cardboard. The string should be longer than the cardboard. Wrap the string around a pencil held at corner B and draw an arc — one fourth of a circle. Using a protractor, mark off the arc in degrees — from zero at B to 90 at C. Tie a weight to the end of the string, and your quadrant is ready to use.

Look at the moon along the top edge of the cardboard, line D-C-A, allowing the string to hang free. When it stops moving, pinch the string to the cardboard and hold it in position. The reading gives you the moon's elevation above the horizon.

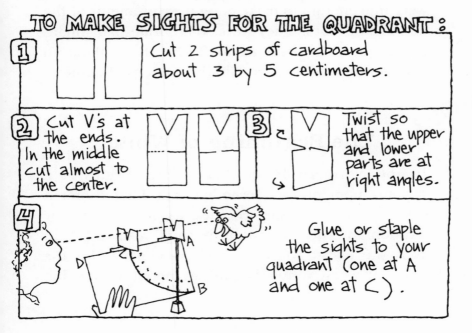

TO MAKE SIGHTS FOR THE QUADRANT:

1 Cut 2 strips of cardboard about 3 by 5 centimeters.

2 Cut V's at the ends. In the middle cut almost to the center.

3 Twist so that the upper and lower parts are at right angles.

4 Glue or staple the sights to your quadrant (one at A and one at C).

"cluck"

If you want to improve your quadrant you can make sights for it. Cut two strips of cardboard about 3 by 5 centimeters. Cut V's at one of the long ends. In the middle make cuts almost to the center. Twist so that the upper and lower sections are at right angles. Glue or staple the sights to your quadrant, one at the point where the string is fastened, the other at the 90-degree mark. You'll find that the V's enable you to sight more accurately. If you want a quadrant that is stronger and so will last longer, you can make one out of plywood or plastic.

Today instruments can measure angles as small as a few thousandths of a degree. They enable astronomers to know the precise positions of objects and to know exactly how they are moving. In the sixteenth century, Tycho couldn't do that, but his quadrants were fine enough to make good measurements of the motions of Mars. They were so accurate that Johannes Kepler, an assistant to Tycho, used them to discover the laws that explain the motions of planets.

The Beginning of Winter

In the Northern Hemisphere winter begins at a certain moment on December 21. That moment comes when the sun reaches its most southerly location. In 1980, that time is 10:56 A.M. (EST), in 1981, 5:51 P.M. You can check an almanac for the moment when winter begins. At noontime on that

day, and on the days just before and after December 21, you may notice that the sun is quite low in the sky. If you were to put a stick into the ground, it would produce a long shadow, the longest noontime shadow of the year. In January the same stick would make a shadow a bit shorter, though the difference would be barely noticeable. However, by March the shadow would be considerably shorter; and in June it would be shortest of all.

During a year the sun appears to move from north to south and back again. Actually, the sun does not move. It is Earth that moves around the sun. Because the axis on which Earth spins is tilted to the path it follows, our angle of view of the sun changes. In winter we in the northern half of the earth are tilted away from the sun. So at noon the sun appears low in the sky. Six months later we are tilted toward the sun, and the noonday sun is high in the sky. It seems that the sun has moved from a low position to a higher one.

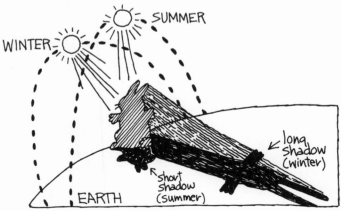

On December 21 the sun is shining directly on the Tropic of Capricorn — a line around the earth that is 23½ degrees south of the equator. Two thousand years ago, when the location was named, the sun was in the constellation Capricorn when winter began. Because of the shifting of the skies, the sun is now in Sagittarius. The sun used to be in Cancer when summer began, and so the earth location where it shines directly on June 21 is called the Tropic of Cancer. Tropic is from a Greek word meaning "turn" — the turning back of the sun.

During winter we have short days and long nights. Look up the times of sunrise and sunset in your newspaper, or in an almanac. If you live at the latitude of Boston, you'll find there are only about 9 hours of daylight — the time between sunrise and sunset — and 15 hours of night. At higher latitudes the days are shorter; nights are longer. On December 21, night at the equator is nearly 12 hours long; at 40 degrees north latitude night lasts 14 hours and 44 minutes; at the North Pole it is 176 days long. For 6 months no sunlight falls on the polar regions.

It takes one year for Earth to make one journey around the sun. During that year, the earth covers 936 000 000 kilometers at an average speed of 105 600 kilometers an hour — 30 times faster than a bullet. That is an average of 1776 kilometers a minute; 29 792 meters a second.

When Earth is closest to the sun, it moves fastest. In January Earth moves 30 286 meters a second. In July it moves more slowly — about 29 310 meters a second. Because of the greater speed during the winter months, the winter season is seven days shorter than the summer season. If you long for warm weather, be patient. Winter is a short season. The sun will soon get higher in the sky, days will get longer, and the northern half of earth will warm up again.

December 11, 1901 — Guglielmo Marconi succeeded in sending a radio signal across the Atlantic Ocean.

December 17, 1903 — The Wright brothers flew their airplane at Kitty Hawk, North Carolina.

December 21 — Long ago people were alarmed to see the sun getting lower in the sky. They feared that it might disappear altogether. However, the sun always reversed itself and reached higher locations. Therefore, December 21 became a time for rejoicing; the sun had reached its lowest position. In following days it would move upward; once more the earth would become warm and crops would grow. December 21 is called the winter solstice from two Latin words — *sol* ("sun") and *sistere* ("stand"). The sun stands still — it moves no lower in the sky.

JANUARY

The first month in the modern calendar has 31 days. January was named after Janus, the two-headed Roman god, because it was the time for looking ahead into the future, and also for looking into the past. Janus was also the god concerned with the beginnings of events. The month was ushered in by offerings of grain meal, frankincense, and wine.

The Anglo-Saxons called the month *wulf-monath,* probably because it was the time wolves were so hungry they came into the villages in search of food.

Northern Lights

In January, as well as in December, February, and March, you may be able to see the northern lights. Look toward the north on a night when the skies are clear and there is no moon. If you live in the northern part of the United States, in Canada, northern Europe or Asia, you may see splashes of bright-colored light in the night sky. Farther south, but still in the Northern Hemisphere, you may see dimmer-colored lights or simply a glow. These are the northern lights, or in Latin the *aurora borealis* — the northern dawn. The display often reminds one of the glow of sunrise or dawn. If you are in the southern half of the world, similar lights may be seen when you look southward. There they are called the *aurora australis* — the southern dawn.

When seen from lower latitudes, the auroras appear as dim lights, or more usually as a glow. Occasionally ripples seem to run through them. As one goes farther north or south of the equator, the auroras become well defined. They display many patterns and are brighter; often there is enough light for one to read a newspaper. Still, the brighter stars can be seen through the filmy light of the aurora. The most usual auroras appear as patches of light, but the type that is most impressive is the curtain or ribbon aurora. In its simplest form the ribbon appears as an arc of color across the sky. As the light develops, fine folds are seen, and the aurora is called a rayed arc. Occasionally the folds are deep. Then the aurora looks like layer after layer of a theater curtain tinged with red along the bottom.

Auroras appear about 80 kilometers above the earth, and they may extend to 800 kilometers. They are produced when electrons and protons from the sun bombard atoms and molecules in the upper atmosphere.

The sun is an active star. Among other things, this means that it ejects electrons and other atomic particles into space. These electrons become part of the solar wind — streams of atomic particles. Those that come near the earth are captured by the planet's magnetic field, the magnetosphere, as it is called.

In many ways Earth behaves like a huge magnet. There is a region or field around a magnet within which objects are attracted. In a similar manner earth has a magnetic field. It extends some 90 000 kilometers into space.

Magnetic lines of force are revealed when a magnet is placed beneath a sheet of paper and iron filings are sprinkled on the paper. The lines seem to originate at the north and south poles of the magnet. Similarly, the lines of force of Earth's magnetic field seem to originate at the polar regions — at the north and south magnetic poles.

Electrons that are free to move tend to follow magnetic lines of force. Electrons from the sun are trapped in our magnetosphere. They flow along the magnetic lines of force and so are directed to the area of the north and south magnetic poles. As they are directed downward toward earth, the electrons collide with atoms and molecules in the upper air. The collisions cause the atoms and molecules to give off light. This is the light of the auroras.

The action is somewhat like that of a television

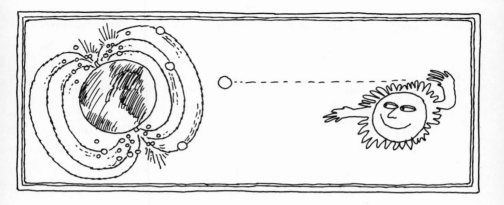

picture tube. At one end of the tube is a source of electrons. The electrons are directed by magnets to the other end of the tube which contains phosphors, chemicals that glow when electrons strike them. In space, electrons are also directed by magnets (the magnetosphere). They are led to the upper atmosphere where the electrons strike atoms, mostly oxygen and nitrogen, that are made to glow by the energy in the electrons.

The colors that are produced vary according to the kind of action that is taking place and whether the atoms are ionized or excited.

The oxygen atom, for example, normally has eight electrons moving around the center. And the electrons move in definite orbits. When bombarded by outside electrons, one or two of the electrons of the atom may be knocked out of the atom. The oxygen atom would then be an oxygen ion. (The atom would be ionized.) The ion seeks to become an atom. It is receptive to receiving electrons and so returning to a normal atom. When the ion takes in an electron, energy is released. That's the light we see in the aurora.

Sometimes the light is produced in another manner. Instead of the atom becoming an ion, the atom is merely excited. It picks up energy but does not lose an electron. In this case electrons are moved to an outer orbit, one that requires more energy. This is not normal, and an atom always "seeks" to become normal. To do so, the electron drops to a lower orbit. In the process the excited atom gives off energy. Some of this energy will be in the form of visible light — the light of the aurora.

Excited oxygen atoms give off green and red light, the color depending upon the amount of energy involved. Ionized nitrogen gives off violet and blue light. On the other hand, excited nitrogen produces deep red.

When auroras occur at low altitudes of 80 to 100 kilometers, the color is mostly green. The usual color of an aurora is soft green, or a greenish yellow. Faint reds usually occur at higher altitudes — 400 to 600 kilometers.

Severe storms occur frequently on the sun. At such times more than the usual amount of particles (electrons and protons) are ejected into the solar wind. A few hours later, aurora displays will be intense and widespread. Normally the aurora is quiet, not active or intense. The increase in intensity shortly after a solar flare-up is extreme. Notice that auroras

Notice that AURORAS occur in the midnight zone—the region directly opposite the sun.

occur in the midnight zone—the region directly opposite the sun.

If you are in a region where they occur quite often, try taking pictures of an aurora. Use high-speed color film. The camera should be wide open. You'll have to experiment with exposure times. Start with 30 seconds, then make shorter exposures of 20, 10, and 5 seconds.

Ben Franklin and Lightning

You don't expect thunderstorms in winter. Usually they occur when it is very hot, in July and August. But thunderstorms can happen in winter. The next time there is a heavy snow storm, you may hear thunder. Chances are you won't see lightning, because it occurs above the low snow clouds.

Back in the eighteenth century Ben Franklin, who was born in Boston on January 17, 1706, wondered about such things. To find out about lightning, he conducted one of the most famous (and most dangerous) of all experiments with lightning.

Franklin wanted to prove that lightning and electricity are the same. To do this, he flew a kite during a lightning storm. The kite had metal wires projecting from the points, and these wires were connected to the kite string. When the kite was flown, the string became wet. Franklin himself was under a wooden shed. He held the kite string with a piece of dry silk cord. Franklin brought his knuckle near to a key that had been fastened to the kite string. A spark jumped from the key to his knuckle. (It's a wonder he wasn't killed, for lightning is a powerful charge of electricity.)

An electric toaster carries a current of 10 to 12 amperes; a lightning stroke may carry 30,000 amperes, even up to 200,000. The voltage of pressure of the stroke is tremendous. One hundred million volts is common, and it may reach a billion or more. (The voltage for the toaster is 110 to 120.) When lightning goes through the air, the air is heated to temperatures that may reach 30,000 degrees Celsius (that's five times hotter than the sun). The temperature is so high that when lightning strikes a tree, it instantly changes water in the tree into steam. The pressure of the steam explodes the tree.

Lightning is a discharge of electricity between clouds, or between a cloud and the ground. Occasionally you may see a glow of "ghost lightning" that looks like the glow of an aurora. It is the light produced by lightning that is far away, perhaps over the horizon. In many ways lightning is similar to the electricity that you often make, either intentionally or accidentally. Scuff across a carpet and then hold your finger near a doorknob. If the weather is dry, a spark may jump from your finger to the doorknob. You have made lightning. Run a comb through your hair and strands of hair will cling to the comb. This too is electricity. Electric charges often build up in clothes dryers; such charges cause the clothes to cling together.

Charges build up because of friction and collisions of water droplets in a storm cloud. The heavier droplets (which are negative — they have excess electrons) tend to fall to the bottom of the cloud. The lighter droplets (those that lack a few electrons) tend to move upward. Therefore the bottom of the storm cloud becomes negatively charged. Air is a poor conductor of these charges, so the charge cannot escape easily. It builds up and up until it "overflows," or discharges.

A slightly luminous channel of free electrons moves in jagged steps from the cloud toward the ground. The channel may be only a few inches across. As the electrons move toward earth, they rip electrons from

25

the atoms in the air. The atoms along the channel are then ionized; they too have lost electrons. When an atom is ionized, it becomes a conductor of electricity.

As soon as the channel reaches the ground, electrons spill out of it to earth, the ones nearest earth spilling first. This leaves a gap immediately above. As electrons spill, the gap moves upward — a stroke of lightning. As electrons move from the cloud to earth, the lightning stroke moves from earth to the cloud. All this takes place in a few thousandths of a second, much too fast for us to see. What we do see is the intensely hot air that has been made white hot by the surge of electricity.

Lightning and thunder occur at the same instant. Light travels very fast — 300 000 kilometers a second — so you see lightning the moment it happens.

Sound travels more slowly — only about 330 meters a second — so it takes about three seconds to go one kilometer.

You can tell how far away a storm is by counting seconds. As soon as you see the lightning, count

seconds by leisurely saying one thousand one, one thousand two, and so on. Keep counting until you hear the thunder. If there are three seconds, the storm is one kilometer away. (If there are five seconds it would be a mile from you.)

ere are some LIGHTNING "DON'TS" to remember:

 DON'T use the telephone - lightning could follow the wire.

 DON'T go under a large tree that stands alone — a grove of trees or a woods is safer.

 DON'T go into a small shed that stands alone.

 DON'T stay in a place where you are taller than your surroundings. DON'T fish from a boat or stand on a hill.

 DON'T carry anything made of metal. DON'T stand near a faucet or anything metal.

LIGHTNING IS DANGEROUS.   RESPECT IT.

January 9, 1793—The first manned balloon flight was made in the United States. A Frenchman, Jean Blanchard, flew from Philadelphia to Cooper's Ferry, New Jersey.

January 10, 1946—The first radar signal was sent to the moon and bounced from the surface.

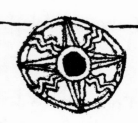

FEBRUARY

The second month of the modern calendar ordinarily has 28 days. In leap years it has 29 days. The name comes from *Februarius,* a Latin word meaning purification. In early days, the Romans held festivals of purification in February; it was a time to correct ills and troubles that may have developed during the year.

Anglo-Saxons called this month *sprout-kale-monath,* because it was the time when cabbage began to grow.

Leap years (when a day is added to February) make it possible for us to keep the calendar in step with the seasons. In one year there are 365 days, 5 hours, 48 minutes, and 46 seconds. That is *nearly* 365 days and 6 hours (one quarter of a day). For three years we ignore this quarter day, but then add a full day every fourth year. But that is 44 minutes and 15 seconds too much. In 100 years it becomes 18 hours and 43 minutes too much. So, every 100 years there is no leap year.

But then we have left out 5 hours and 17 minutes too much. So, every 400 years we put back a day. But that is 2 hours and 48 minutes too much. So every 4000 years we do not add a day. The year 4000 will not be a leap year, even though it is divisible by both 4 and 400. It takes a bit of doing to keep the calendar in agreement with the seasons.

Groundhog Day

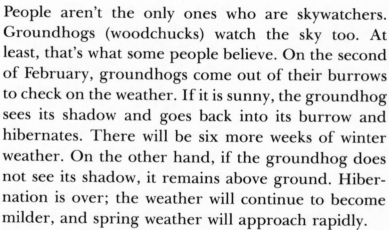

People aren't the only ones who are skywatchers. Groundhogs (woodchucks) watch the sky too. At least, that's what some people believe. On the second of February, groundhogs come out of their burrows to check on the weather. If it is sunny, the groundhog sees its shadow and goes back into its burrow and hibernates. There will be six more weeks of winter weather. On the other hand, if the groundhog does not see its shadow, it remains above ground. Hibernation is over; the weather will continue to become milder, and spring weather will approach rapidly.

That's what weather lore says. The belief originated in Europe. In the Christian world there is a tradition that a sunny Candlemas (the fortieth day after Christmas) will be followed by cold weather. Candlemas (the blessing of the candles) is a religious festival that honors the Mother of Jesus. In Scotland there is a saying: "If Candlemas is fair and clear, there'll be two winters in the year."

We doubt very much that groundhogs can predict the weather. But be sure to check for sunshine (or lack of it) on February 2 and notice whether the next six weeks are cold and wintry, or more springlike.

Perhaps woodchucks are not reliable weather forecasters. But other animals are, or seem to be. People say that squirrels store large amounts of nuts and acorns before an especially cold winter—and they start early. Others say that you can tell if the winter will be cold by the thickness of a horse's winter coat—the heavier the coat, the colder the winter.

Maybe so. It might be fun to find out more weather traditions like these, and to see if they really do tell anything about future weather.

Galileo and the Moons of Jupiter

Galileo, the famous Italian scientist who was born February 15, 1564, is known for many discoveries, such as the rings of Saturn, the mountains on the moon, the phases of Venus, and the moons of Jupiter. If you have a pair of binoculars, 7 by 50 or better, you should be able to see four of the moons of Jupiter just as Galileo saw them almost four hundred years ago.

First, you'll have to find out where to look. Check your local newspaper, where there may be a listing of the planets that are visible. Or turn to an almanac, or magazines such as *Natural History* or *Sky and Telescope.* They list the planets that can be seen during every month of the year. Once you have determined Jupiter's location, you can find a rather bright object that appears to glow steadily. Look at it through binoculars (or a telescope if you have one).

Very likely you will find it impossible to keep the binoculars steady. To do this, you should clamp the glasses to a chair back. Clamps for holding binoculars can usually be bought at a camera shop. If the binoculars are powerful enough and if they are steady, you should be able to see four of Jupiter's thirteen moons. They will appear as small points of light alongside the planet. All four may be on one side, or they may be separated — some east of the planet and the others west of it. If one or more of the moons are directly in front of Jupiter, or behind it, they will of course be invisible.

Make a sketch that shows the satellites and their locations relative to Jupiter. The next night make another sketch. Do this for several weeks and you'll discover, just as Galileo did, that the moons move around the planet.

In order of their periods of revolution, the four Galilean moons of Jupiter are Io, Europa, Ganymede, and Callisto. The periods range from 42 hours for Io to 16 days and 16 hours for Callisto.

The word *moon* should be used for only one body in the solar system, earth's satellite. The "moons" of all the other planets are properly called satellites. There are thirty-four in the solar system. Thirteen of these belong to Jupiter. For almost three hundred years people believed Jupiter had only four satellites. Since 1892 nine more have been discovered, the last one in 1974. And in 1979 astronomers discovered that Jupiter has rings very much like those of Saturn and Uranus, although they are difficult to observe.

Nicholas Copernicus and Sky Motions

As you look into the February skies, notice that all the stars seem to be the same distance from us. We seem to be inside a ball on which the stars are placed, and the ball seems to be turning, producing star-rise and star-set.

It is easy to understand why for centuries people believed Earth stood still, and the sky turned. Not only did the stars rise and set, but so did the sun, the moon, and the planets; one could see that they turned around the earth. Motions of the sun, moon, and planets were different from those of the stars. To explain these motions, the ancients supposed that the objects were going around the earth in paths inside the sphere of stars. Those that went around in the least time — the moon, Mercury, Venus, and the sun — were close to Earth. Those that took longer — Mars, Jupiter, and Saturn — were farther away.

As you look at the skies, think of these explanations

and you will see why they seemed logical. It really does appear that earth is standing still, for you cannot feel any motion; movement of the sky objects around us could account for all the changes that we see.

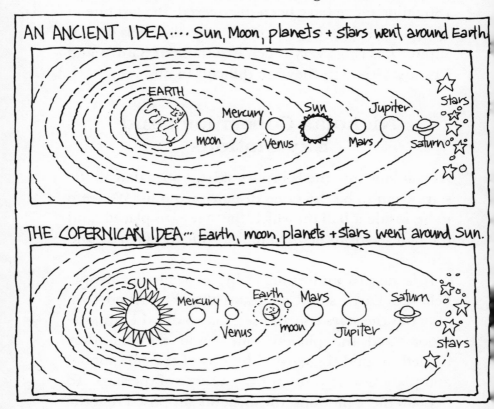

Nicholas Copernicus, who was born in Poland on February 19, 1473, made a bold stroke. He said that all the motions of the sun, moon, planets, and stars could be explained by supposing earth itself was moving. Earth spins from west to east, he said, and so stars rise as we are carried toward them. They set as we turn away from them. And so it is for other objects that rise and set.

During the centuries since then, as more was learned about the solar system, the ideas of Copernicus were proved over and over again to be correct. Today, there are few if any people who do not accept them.

As you skywatch, keep in mind that you are on a moving platform. It helps you to understand many of the events that occur in the sky.

February 4, 1902—Charles A. Lindbergh, the first man to fly alone (in 1927) from the United States to France, was born.

February 9, 1870—The weather service was established by Congress as a part of the Army Signal Corps, and official weather record keeping began.

February 18, 1930—Clyde W. Tombaugh located Pluto, the ninth planet in the solar system.

February 20, 1967—John H. Glenn became the first American to go into orbit around the earth inside a Mercury capsule.

The Spring Stars

Looking southward about 9 P.M. toward the middle of April you will see the stars of spring. Dominating the sky is Regulus, a fairly bright star. Just above it are five dimmer stars arranged like a backward question mark. They are all part of the constellation Leo, the Lion. In March, Leo is east of south, and in May it is west of south.

Regulus, the heart of the lion, is 84 light years away. It is a hundred times brighter than the sun. The stars above Regulus are considered to indicate the lion's head.

A bit east of Regulus you will see three stars that make a triangle. These are the hindquarter of the lion. The last of the three stars, Denebola, marks the lion's tail.

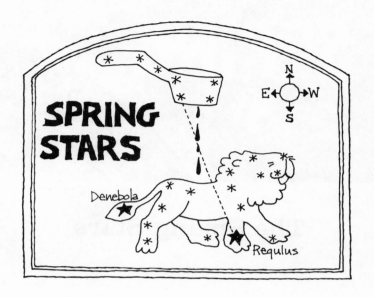

Northward from Regulus is the Big Dipper. Some people locate Leo by first finding the Dipper and then, supposing there were a hole in it, following the direction of the leaking liquid to Leo.

Regulus is almost on the ecliptic, the path that the sun follows in the course of a year. A bit east and south of Denebola the ecliptic crosses the celestial equator, the line that divides the sky into the northern and southern halves. When the sun is at that location, fall begins.

MARCH

The third month of the modern calendar contains 31 days. In the ancient Roman calendar March was the first month of the year. In England, March was the first month until it was changed to month number three in 1752. The month is named for Mars, the Roman god of war.

Anglo-Saxons called March *hlyd-monath,* which means loud and stormy month. It was also called *lencten-monath,* or lengthening month. This was because in March days got longer rapidly, after the shorter, cold days of winter.

First Day of Spring

Spring begins when the sun is directly above the equator. At that moment a person at the right location on the equator would see the sun directly overhead; it would be at his zenith. This occurs on or about March 21. The time of day depends where on the earth you happen to be. East of that location on the equator, the time would be after noon; west of that location the time would be in the morning.

On the first day of spring the sun is at the vernal equinox. (*Vernal* is the Latin word for spring, and *equinox* — "equal nights" — also comes from two Latin words.) It is the time when days and nights are of equal length around the world — just about 12 hours each. The vernal equinox is a location in the sky where the ecliptic (the sun's path) crosses the celestial equator. Presently they cross in the part of the sky where the constellation Pisces is located.

During the six months after the first day of spring, the sun will be north of the celestial equator, the equator that divides the sky into two halves, northern and southern.

In the Northern Hemisphere, days will gradually become longer, and the nights shorter. In the Arctic region there will soon be 24 hours of daylight. Just the opposite conditions will prevail in the Southern Hemisphere. There the days will become shorter, and the nights longer. Antarctica will be entering the period of continuous darkness, the sun being below the horizon 24 hours a day.

On the first day of spring, the sun rises directly east and sets due west. At noontime (Standard Time) the sun's elevation — its angle above the horizon — is the colatitude. To find your latitude, subtract it from 90 degrees.

You can check this yourself:

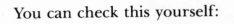

On March 21 put a stick in the ground so the sun will shine on it at noontime. Make sure the stick is vertical by lining it up with a piece of string hanging free with a weight on the end.

At noontime, put a mark at the tip of the shadow of the stick.

Tack a string to the top of the stick.

Stretch the string to the mark.

Measure the angle that the string makes with the ground.

To find latitude, subtract from 90°.

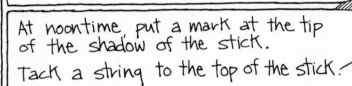

OR YOU COULD GET THE ANGLE THIS WAY:

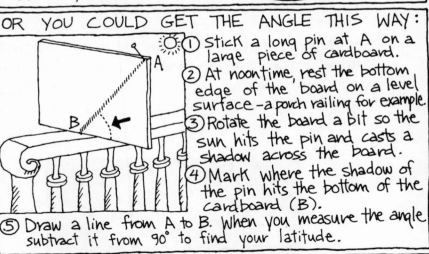

① Stick a long pin at A on a large piece of cardboard.

② At noontime, rest the bottom edge of the board on a level surface – a porch railing for example.

③ Rotate the board a bit so the sun hits the pin and casts a shadow across the board.

④ Mark where the shadow of the pin hits the bottom of the cardboard (B).

⑤ Draw a line from A to B. When you measure the angle subtract it from 90° to find your latitude.

The Man in the Moon

March is a good season to observe the moon, for it is fairly high in the sky—just as high as the noontime sun. However, its features can also be seen in other seasons, any time when the moon is full.

In observing some sky objects, the constellations, for example, it is helpful to use your imagination. It is difficult to see a lion in the stars of Leo, twin figures in Gemini, or a dog in the stars of Canis Major. However, imagination helps you to fill in the general outlines. And so it is with the man in the moon.

The light and dark parts of the moon—the plains and mountains—suggest various creatures to different people. The next time you see the full moon, look closely and you may be able to see the eyes, nose, and mouth of the man (or woman) in the moon. That's what the lights and shadows suggest to many people in different parts of the world.

In Japan people do not see the moon that way. When they observe the moon they see a rabbit in profile. It is sitting on its haunches and facing eastward. Two long rabbit ears extend westward along the northern part of the moon. If you forget

about the man in the moon, and think of a rabbit, you may be able to see the rabbit.

In Scandinavian countries people see neither a man nor a rabbit. They see a boy and girl, just as they have for centuries. They made the characters, and their changing appearance, into a nursery rhyme that has become "Jack and Jill" in the English language. When the moon is approaching first quarter, the people see Jack appear. As the days pass and the moon grows, Jill is revealed.

> Jack and Jill went up a hill
> To fetch a pail of water.

When the moon is full, both Jack and Jill can be seen. Between them they hold a pail of water.

As the month progresses, the full moon decreases. Jack disappears, followed by Jill.

> Jack fell down and broke his crown,
> And Jill came tumbling after.

Use your imagination, and you may also see Jack and Jill appear and disappear with changes in the size of the moon.

Jack and Jill went up the hill to fetch a pail of water...

Jack fell down And broke his crown...

And Jill came tumbling after!

The connection between the Jack-and-Jill story and the changing moon arose because people relate weather to the moon. They say that when the moon is growing, changing from new moon to full, the weather is dry: Jack and Jill go to fetch water. As the moon gets smaller, as it changes from full to new, the weather tends to be rainy: Jack and Jill fall and drop the pail of water.

You may find it interesting to see if there is any truth to the belief. Keep track of the moon phases and the periods of dry and rainy weather for as many months as you can. You may find that the Scandinavians are right, that the moon and the weather change together.

March 13, 1781 — Using a telescope he had built, Sir William Herschel discovered the planet Uranus. In all his work, Herschel was helped a great deal by his sister, Caroline. She ground lenses for the telescope, kept records, and made star maps. On her own, Caroline Herschel discovered eight comets and three nebulae, and completed Herschel's star catalogue after his death.

FLOWERS OPEN

APRIL

The fourth month of the modern calendar has 30
days. In Roman times it was the second month of the
year. The name comes from the Latin word *aperiere*,
which means to open. April is the time when leaves
open, and flowers bloom.

In Rome, April 21 was regarded as the birthday of
the city. It was a time of wine tasting and celebrations.

Sun Dogs and Sun Halos

Sometimes when the sun is low in the sky, you can see
three suns: the main one and smaller, less bright suns
on either side. Often there will be other "suns" above

and below as well—five suns altogether. These images of the sun are called sun dogs—mock, or false, suns. The name probably comes from the verb "to dog," that is, to follow closely. Sun dogs "follow" the sun in many months of the year. But the spring, when there are frequent showers and water droplets and ice crystals in the air, is the best time to see them.

Mock suns form when there is a halo around the sun. Under certain conditions you may see the halo, a ring around the sun. The inside of the ring will be somewhat reddish. When you see a halo, or a sun dog, you'll notice that there are high, thin clouds. They are called cirrus or cirrostratus clouds. *Cirro* means curled and *stratus* means layers. The lower level of the clouds is 5 or 6 kilometers high where temperature is well below freezing. The clouds are thin and whitish and often cover the sky completely, giving it a milky appearance. At other times the clouds are somewhat broken and so produce weblike formations. They are always thin enough so the sun (or the moon) shines through them. In daytime the halo can be seen better if you hold your hand in front of the sun to reduce the glare.

Halos are caused by ice crystals in these cirrus clouds. The crystals reflect light—light bounces off the surface of the crystals; and they also refract light—light enters the crystal and comes out at a different angle. The halos are always at definite angles from the sun. The first one, which is seen most often, is 22 degrees from the sun. The second ring,

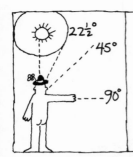

To estimate 22° stand facing the sun. Extend your right arm sideways. This gives a 90° angle with your line of sight toward the sun. Half of that is 45° and half of that angle is 22½°.

which is much dimmer and much harder to see, is 46 degrees from the sun. Frequently the halos show colors similar to those in a rainbow, reddish on the inside and blending through yellow to blue-white on the outside.

When sky conditions are such that halos form, they also produce a line of light at the level of the sun going all around the sky. This is called the parhelic circle. (*Par* is from a Greek word meaning beside, and *helic* is from *helios*, the Greek word for sun.) The circle is produced by reflection of sunlight. Sun dogs appear where a halo intersects the parhelic circle. Another term for sun dog is *parhelion*—an image beside the sun. Sometimes the halo is obscured and only the sun dogs can be seen. If both the halo and sun dogs are visible the sun dogs will be a bit outside the halo. The outer sun dogs, those formed at the second halo, are seen only rarely. However, the inner images are distinct. If you keep watching the sun as it moves toward the horizon and shines through cirrus clouds, sooner or later conditions will be just right for you to see sun dogs.

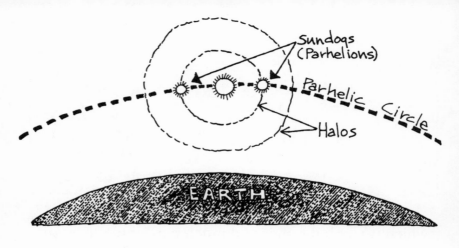

As the sun moves toward the horizon, angles change slightly. This may cause the sun dogs to move slightly outside the halo. The effect is to give them "flaming tails." People who do not understand the cause of them have attached all sorts of mystic explanations to these flaming sun dogs. Usually they are thought to be omens of disaster: great fires will engulf the world, disease will spread around the world, or the world will soon come to an end.

Halos were first explained by René Descartes (1596–1650), one of the most famous French scholars and scientists. His explanation, made more than 300 years ago, is the one given above: halos are effects caused by ice crystals in the path of sunlight.

You don't have to have any special skills to see sun dogs or halos. However, the same conditions that produce the dogs and halos often produce other light streaks which skilled observers look for. The different streaks and arcs are produced by ice crystals at slightly varying angles, and crystals that have different edges turned toward the observer.

Moon Dogs and Moon Halos

The explanations for sun dogs and halos also apply to the moon. Because moonlight is less brilliant than sunlight, moon dogs and halos are usually less well defined. However, because of the dimmer light, the moon produces less glare. This makes the moon halo easier to see.

According to some observers, a halo around the sun or the moon is a sign that there will soon be rain. Like many weather sayings, this one has an element of truth.

A halo results because of the presence of cirrus clouds. They may be wispy, or better defined into layers or clumps. Very often these thin, wispy clouds will become more heavily laden with moisture. Then their elevation will decrease, the ice crystals will melt, and the cirrostratus clouds will become heavier, darker, lower altostratus clouds. These clouds often bring scattered showers.

Some observers say that to know when it will rain, all one need do is count the stars inside the ring around the moon. The number of stars will indicate the number of days before it will rain.

What do you think? Whenever you see a moon halo, count the stars inside it and keep track of the weather. If it rains shortly after you see a halo, you can judge whether the number of stars inside the halo indicates the days before rainfall.

Phases of the Moon

The moon is an excellent object for skywatchers to observe. In fact, a skywatcher who observes the moon exclusively will find plenty of challenges. Perhaps most apparent are the phases of the moon—changes in its apparent shape.

In ancient times people knew why these changes occurred. And certainly Galileo knew when he observed Venus at the start of the seventeenth century. Using his newly built telescope, he found that Venus went through a complete cycle of changes, just as did the moon. It was apparent from his observations that these changes occurred because Venus went around the sun. As you can see from the drawing, if Venus did not go around the sun (as many believed), there could be no complete cycle of phase changes. The planet would change somewhat, but there could never be a full Venus.

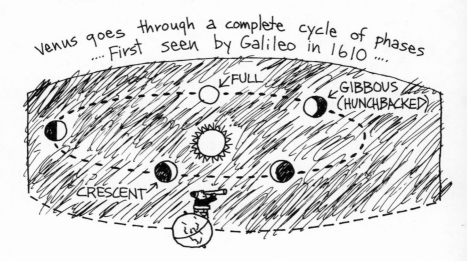

Venus goes through a complete cycle of phases .... First seen by Galileo in 1610 ....

FULL
GIBBOUS (HUNCHBACKED)
CRESCENT

The moon goes through phases because it revolves around the earth, because one half of it is always illuminated by the sun (except briefly during lunar eclipses when the earth shadows the moon) and because we see varying amounts of the lighted half.

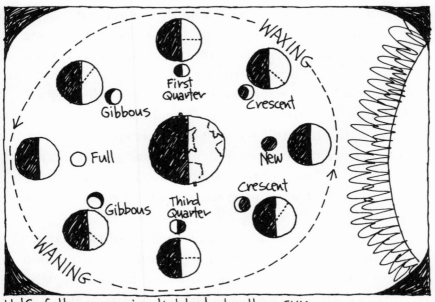

Half of the moon is lighted by the sun.
We see varying amounts of the lighted half.

When the moon is between the sun and earth, the moon is new. It cannot be seen from Earth. However, a few hours later the first thin moon sliver or crescent can be seen. You may want to find the earliest you can see this new crescent. Check your calendar to see when the moon will be new. Better, check an almanac, which will give you the time of the new moon, as well as the date.

Beginning about 12 hours later, watch the western sky for the crescent. This is what ancient priests did. The moment a sighting was made, the event was announced. And so a new month was started.

Hour by hour the moon grows. It is a waxing (growing) moon. About a week later, the crescent has become a first-quarter moon.

Beyond a quarter moon, the moon develops a bulge. It is called a gibbous (hunchbacked) moon.

The moon is full when it is about two weeks old. Then, once more it becomes gibbous; it grows smaller and so is called a waning moon. Three weeks after it first appeared, the moon has reached the last-quarter phase.

It diminishes to a crescent that steadily becomes smaller. After a bit more than four weeks, the moon is once more new and again invisible from the earth.

Watch the phases for a month or so. Sketch the changing moon and also the background stars. If you

Full Moon   Waning Gibbous   Third Quarter   Waning Crescent

make sketches for two or three consecutive days, you will discover that the moon moves quite a lot from one day to the next. It changes position relative to the background stars. In one month the moon goes around the earth; it moves through 360 degrees. That means each day the moon moves through 12 degrees. Your sketches will give you a sense of 12 degrees in the sky. (The space between the pointer stars of the Big Dipper is 5 degrees.) To cover this distance, the moon moves about 3600 kilometers an hour.

The moon's journey around earth is completed in about 28 days—to be exact, in 27 days, 7 hours, 43 minutes, 11.5 seconds. This is called the sidereal, or star, period.

A sidereal period is the time required for the earth and moon to realign with a distant star. At new moon, for example, the earth, moon, and sun are in line—so also is one particular star. After 27⅓ days, the earth, moon, and the same star are once more in line. (The star is so far away that its light is always parallel no matter where earth is in its orbit.)

But your calendar or almanac shows a different

New Moon   Waxing Crescent   First Quarter   Waxing Gibbous

time, one that is closer to 30 days — again, to be exact, 29 days, 12 hours, 44 minutes, 2.8 seconds. This is the synodic period, or the time from a phase to a repeat of the same phase — from full moon to the next full moon, for example.

The word *synod* means a gathering. In this case it refers to the "gathering" of the sun, earth, and moon.

While the moon goes around Earth, Earth is going around the sun. About two days are needed for the moon to get in line between the earth and the sun and

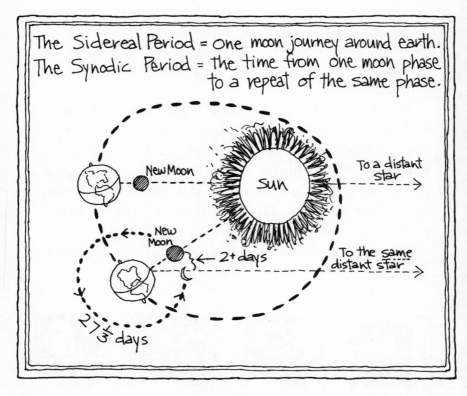

for the moon once again to appear new. This longer time is the synodic period.

Skywatch the moon — not only its phases but also other changes. For example, changes in sky location which vary with the seasons; changes in color caused by changes in our atmosphere; and apparent changes in the size of the moon as it moves from moonrise to moonset. The moon is a skywatcher's delight.

April 12, 1961 — Yuri Gagarin, the Russian cosmonaut, became the first person to travel in space around the earth. His flight lasted 108 minutes.

MAY

The fifth month of our calendar has 31 days. It was the third month in the Roman calendar. May is named for the Roman goddess Maia, daughter of the god Atlas. It was a time of celebration.

In England the first day of May was a public holiday. People went out into the country and returned with branches, leaves, and flowers. The center of activity was a Maypole hung with wreaths and ribbons. What was perhaps the all-time highest Maypole was set up in 1661 in London. The Duke of York, who later became King James II, put up, with the help of 21 sailors, a pole that was 134 feet high.

Comets

In 1986 you should be able to see Halley's comet. Right now it is moving closer in its journey around the sun, a trip that takes 76 years to complete. When last seen, in 1910, the comet had a tail 150 million miles long. In 1986 it may be just as long.

Between now and then there may be other comets for you to see; several are discovered every year and old comets make return visits. If there is one, newspapers and television will give reports about it, and tell you where to see it.

Pictures of comets show long, streaming tails which give the impression that the comet is moving very fast. And so it is, but the comet is far away and the motion is not apparent to skywatchers. A comet appears to be hanging in the sky; it seems to be a fuzzy, starlike object. With binoculars you can see the "tail." As a comet approaches the sun, the tail trails behind the head of the comet. As it moves away from the sun, the tail goes before the head of the comet, like the beam of a flashlight. This is because the solar wind (particles ejected from the sun) pushes gases and particles away from the head of a comet; the closer to the sun, the longer the tail.

Halley's comet is named after Edmund Halley, an English astronomer who saw the comet in 1682. He studied its orbit and believed the comet would return later on. He predicted it would return in 1759, and it did. Halley had proved that comets move in orbits around the sun.

Comets usually are named after the people who

discover them. One person, Kaoru Ikeya, has five comets named after him, either alone, or jointly with a codiscoverer. He found his first comet when he was 19 years old, using a telescope that he made himself.

Another Japanese skywatcher is Tsutomu Seki, who lived only about 240 miles from Ikeya. In 1967 they separately discovered a comet. Since the discoveries were close together, the comet is now called the Ikeya-Seki 1967 VII. To classify a comet, the year of discovery is given; the Roman numeral is the order in which the comet passes close to the sun; Ikeya-Seki was the seventh comet to do so in that year.

It used to be that most new comets were discovered by amateurs who scanned the sky with small telescopes. Professional astronomers used their big telescopes to study stars and galaxies — to make specific observations. There was not enough time to search the sky for a fuzzy object that might turn out to be a new comet.

Presently, however, most comets are discovered by professionals. Large sections of the sky are photographed by astronomers in observatories. Their telescopes are powerful, so small details show up in the photographs. The photographs are scanned in a laboratory and anything unusual is noticed.

When Halley's comet returns in 1986 it will be the thirtieth time the comet has been seen. Skywatchers hope that it will be bright, and that a long tail will develop. However, chances are that it will be dimmer than it was in 1910. Each time a comet moves closer to the sun, the gravitation of the sun pulls out some of the gas and dust in the comet. The comet gets smaller and less bright. Watch your newspaper for news about Halley's comet, and also new comets that may become visible. Very likely a comet probe will be launched to intercept Halley's comet. Instruments aboard will determine the materials in the head of the comet, and also those that are in the tail.

Rachel Carson and Pollution

Pollution of air, water, and soil is with us every month of the year. It affects many aspects of our lives. One of the first people to speak out against pollution was Rachel Carson, who was born on May 4, 1907. In her book, *Silent Spring,* she led a fight to get rid of the pollution caused by insecticides. Another form of pollution that concerned her is the smog that gathers in the sky over big cities. This air pollution causes many different kinds of problems. For skywatchers it means that observations are difficult to make. One of the problems is light. If you're near a city or town you know what we mean. Night viewing is best when there are no artificial lights to make the sky glow and reduce visibility. When those lights are over a city whose skies are hazy, the problem is even greater. Professional astronomers must go to places far removed from city lights and haze to make their observations. Either that, or they must turn to infrared or radio astronomy rather than optical (visible light) astronomy. Infrared and radio waves go through haze, so infrared pictures are much sharper than photographs taken in visible light.

Particles in the air are another kind of pollution. They are smoke and soot, and also pollen grains which exist almost everywhere. You can collect particles by smearing a plate with oil or petroleum jelly. Leave the plate in an exposed place for a day or so to see what you pick up. (Probably you'll also catch some insects, but they're not really pollution particles.) At the start of a rainstorm or snowstorm, put a dish outside. You may be surprised at how many particles are "washed" out of the air during the first few minutes of the storm.

If you've ever been in smog you know firsthand about another kind of air pollution. Smog is a mixture of fog and smoke and exhaust from cars. Smog makes it hard to breathe, and people who are sick are especially uncomfortable. Cars, electric generating plants, and factories all pollute the air. They give off carbon monoxide, sulfur and nitrogen compounds, and hydrocarbons. Some of these we are not aware of. But the gases become dangerous when they are trapped in low areas, as often happens around many cities. There are no air movements to carry them away.

Cars and coal fires give off chemicals that become

acids when they mix with water in clouds. When it rains, these weak acids fall to earth. They may kill fish in ponds and change soil so crops do not grow well on it. Acid rain is a great worry to many scientists, and ways must be found to reduce it.

Because of pollution, observatories in Europe, Asia, and North America are built atop high mountains and far from city lights. But even this doesn't solve the problem. Several universities have their observatories in South America in the high Andes Mountains, where the air is especially free of pollution. Most skywatchers can't travel to such distant places. If there is a lot of pollution where you live, you can still skywatch. You should be able to see the brighter stars and planets, the moon and its phases, and shadows and the way they change from morning to afternoon and from season to season.

May 5, 1961 — Alan B. Shepard, Jr., made the first U.S. space flight. His flight of 19 minutes took him 116 miles (185.6 km) into space.

May 18, 1910 — Earth passed through the tail of Halley's comet. In spite of predictions of great calamities, nothing happened; the gases in the tail were too thin to be noticed.

The Summer Stars

During the summer months twilight brightens the evening sky so you must start skywatching a bit later. About 10:00 P.M. toward the end of July, when the day has darkened, look southward. Quite high up you will see an especially bright star, which is Vega in the constellation Lyra. Alongside Vega, on the eastern side of it, you will see four dimmer stars that make a crooked rectangle; they are also part of Lyra.

East of Vega and a bit above it is Deneb, and below Deneb is Altair. All three stars are quite bright. Together they make the summer triangle.

Deneb and the stars below it are in the constellation Cygnus, the Swan. Some people call the formation the Northern Cross. Deneb is the top of the upright of the cross. Perhaps you can imagine the cross more easily than a flying swan.

63

Altair, the third star in the triangle, is in the constellation Aquila, the Eagle. Your imagination has to strain to see a bird here—an eagle or any other kind of creature.

Earlier in the summer the triangle is shifted toward the east; later it is toward the west.

You'll notice that the Dipper is high in the sky and toward the west. It seems to be standing on its handle.

THE DRY MONTH

JUNE

The sixth month in our calendar has 30 days. The month had only 29 days until Julius Caesar added a day to it in 46 B.C. The name comes from Juno, the queen of the Roman gods.

Anglo-Saxons called June the dry month. It is the month when summer begins.

The Start of Summer

June 21, the longest day of the year, is also the day when the noonday sun is highest in the sky, and when shadows are the shortest.

Summer begins when the sun reaches the summer solstice. *Solstice* means the sun stands still. Since spring, the noonday sun has been moving higher. After June 21 the noonday sun will be moving lower. At the start of summer the sun "stands still"—it moves neither higher nor lower in the sky. The solstice is a point in the sky located in the constellation Gemini. It is the most northerly location of the sun. At noontime, the sun is high in the sky. To determine how high it is, you must know your latitude. Subtract your latitude from 90 degrees, and add 23½ degrees to the difference. The answer will be the angle of the sun above the horizon on the first day of summer.

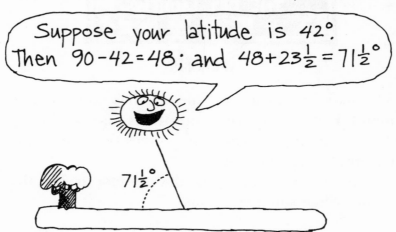

In the latitude of the United States, the sun is never directly overhead, at 90 degrees, that is. The only part of the world where the sun ever gets directly overhead is the Torrid Zone. The boundaries of the zone are 23½ degrees north and south of the equator. Suppose you lived 23½ degrees north of the equator; then, following the formula: $90 - 23½ = 66½$; and $66½ + 23½ = 90$.

There are ways of checking the angle of the sun. One way was suggested earlier under March. Here is another way, using a stick and a piece of cardboard.

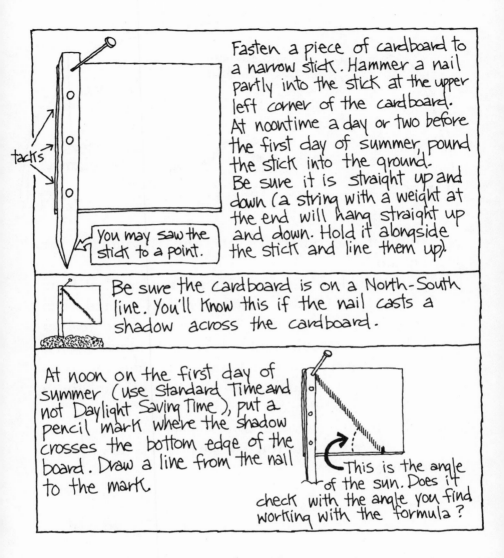

Fasten a piece of cardboard to a narrow stick. Hammer a nail partly into the stick at the upper left corner of the cardboard. At noontime a day or two before the first day of summer, pound the stick into the ground. Be sure it is straight up and down (a string with a weight at the end will hang straight up and down. Hold it alongside the stick and line them up).

tacks

You may saw the stick to a point.

Be sure the cardboard is on a North-South line. You'll know this if the nail casts a shadow across the cardboard.

At noon on the first day of summer (use Standard Time and not Daylight Saving Time), put a pencil mark where the shadow crosses the bottom edge of the board. Draw a line from the nail to the mark.

This is the angle of the sun. Does it check with the angle you find working with the formula?

In the same manner you can measure the angle of the sun at other times of the year. From spring to fall, you add 23½ degrees to the difference that you get when you subtract your latitude from 90 degrees (the sun is north of the equator). From fall to spring, you

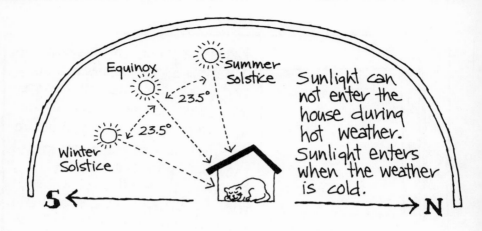

subtract the difference (the sun is south of the equator).

The angle of the sun changes a great deal from summer to winter. Architects keep this in mind when they design buildings. In summer, when the weather is hot, most people want to keep sunlight out of their house. But in winter they want it to shine in. To do this they often build a roof that cuts off sunlight in summer, but admits it in winter.

During the course of a year check the angle of the sun where you live. You'll be surprised at how much it changes.

Sunburn

June, July, and August are the sunburn months. Of course sun shines at other times of the year, but these are the months when most of us spend time in the sun. Also, these are the times when the sun is highest in the northern sky. It is the time when sunlight passes through less atmosphere. A greater amount of ultraviolet light reaches us, and therefore we are more apt to get sunburned.

The sun is an energy factory. Deep in its interior, where the temperature is some 14 000 000 degrees, nuclear reactions are occurring, helium is being produced from hydrogen, and energy is being released. Each second 564 000 000 tons of hydrogen react. Of this total, 560 000 000 tons become helium and 4 000 000 tons are converted into energy.

All forms of energy are produced: radio waves, infrared waves, visible light, ultraviolet light, x rays, and gamma rays. All of these are forms of electromagnetic radiation. They travel 300 000 kilometers a second (the speed of light) and they travel in waves.

The length of the waves gets shorter as one goes from radio waves to visible light, ultraviolet, and so on. Visible light has a wave length between 380 and 760 nanometers. (A nanometer [nm] is one billionth of a meter.) The longest waves produce red light and the shortest give us violet light. Waves shorter than 380 nm are ultra (beyond) violet. Fortunately most of the ultraviolet radiation does not reach us. The atmosphere filters out the shortest waves, x rays and short-wave ultraviolet. The longer wave ultraviolet light can penetrate through the atmosphere around noon when thickness of the atmosphere is not too great. It is this long or medium wave ultraviolet radiation that produces sunburn.

If you ski, you know that sunburn is not limited to June, July, and August. At high altitudes a person burns quickly because the air is thinner. There is less air to filter out the ultraviolet light. Also, snow reflects the light. And, if you are high enough, the light comes from an entire half of the sky, from all directions. However, the sunburn you get while skiing is usually not severe because most of your body is covered.

Sand on the beach also reflects light. And, if the beach is flat, the light comes from all directions. When you're at the beach, a breeze cools you. People do not realize how hot the sun is, and they feel that they can stay in the sun as long as they want. But if your skin is not already tanned, ten or twenty minutes is the longest you should be exposed to summer sun. In following days you can lengthen the time. Take it easy; give your skin time to build its own natural protection.

The main defense of the skin against sunburn is melanin, which all of us have. This is the brown pigment or coloring material of the skin. Melanin combines with those skin cells that produce keratin, the outer layer of the skin. The amount of melanin you have, or produce when exposed to the sun, and its distribution in the keratin determine the color of your skin.

There is a lot of melanin in tanned skin, or in skin that is naturally dark. When a person is exposed to ultraviolet light, the skin may tan very fast without burning. This is because melanin combines with oxygen when ultraviolet light is present and it darkens. A more permanent tan follows because the ultraviolet light causes a gradual increase in the amount of melanin. This takes four or five days, or often a week or more. A good layer of melanin in the outer skin protects the underskin from about 90 percent of ultraviolet light. However, melanin is not the only preventive, for many dark-skinned people suffer from sunburn. Other substances in the skin also provide protection, among them the keratin.

The redness of sunburn comes from an enlargement of the blood vessels just below the outer skin layer. The enlargement allows a greater flow of blood, producing the redness and also increasing skin temperature.

The outer layer of your skin is constantly flaking off and new cells are replacing the old ones. All is balanced, so the outer layer remains the same thickness. In sunburned people this action is interrupted. The process of cell replacement becomes more rapid, reaching a peak about three days after exposure. The outer layer of the skin becomes much thicker, and it may remain so for the rest of the summer. Continued exposure may cause this outer layer to build up a considerable thickness, and it may last several months. In certain fair-skinned people who spend a great deal of time in the sun, this abnormal growth of cells often results in skin cancer.

Ultraviolet light can cause severe sunburn, so be

sensible when you go out in the sun. Stay out in it for only a short time at first, or cover up if you must stay out longer than ten or twenty minutes. But don't stay out of the sun altogether. Sunshine is good for you. It enables your body to produce vitamin D, without which your bones would not develop properly. However, only 5 percent of the sunlight required to produce a sunburn is enough for this purpose.

When you are skiing, sunshine is good for another reason: it keeps you warm even though the air temperature may be very cold. And for many of us the best vacation is one that includes a few warm, sleepy days basking on the beach, enjoying all the benefits of the sun, including its ultraviolet light, and getting sunburned, a little at a time.

June 29, 1868—George Ellery Hale was born. He invented many different astronomical instruments. The 200-inch telescope on Mount Palomar is called the Hale telescope in his honor and because he did much of the designing of the instrument.

June 16, 1963—Valentina V. Tereshkova, the first woman to go into outer space, climbed aboard the Soviet spaceship Vostok 6 and made 48 orbits around the earth. The mission kept her in space 70 hours and 50 minutes.

JULY

The seventh month has 31 days. Originally the month was called Quintilis, the fifth month of the year. The modern name comes from Julius Caesar, who was born in this month. The name came into use in 44 B.C., the year of Julius Caesar's death.

Anglo-Saxons called July *heg-monath* ("hay month") or *maed-monath* ("mead month") the time when flowers bloomed in the meadows.

The Green Flash

If you are a patient skywatcher, and one who knows when and where to look, you may be lucky enough to see the green flash, a bright green strip of light that appears just above the setting sun. Usually it is seen close to the horizon an instant after the sun itself has disappeared, and it lasts for only a moment. It can be seen at other times of the year too, but July is one of the best times to look for it, because you may be at the seashore or in the mountains on vacation.

For the green flash to be seen, the horizon must be sharp and clear of haze. These are conditions most likely to occur over water, on mountains, or in deserts. The desert area of Egypt is an especially good place. The ancient Egyptians knew about the flash. Often they represented the sun as a half-circle colored blue and green. Early Egyptians thought that during the night the sun was green. They probably got the idea from seeing the green flash at sunset.

If there is a sharp horizon where you live, one without haze, watch the sun as it sets. Just after it disappears you may see a narrow strip of bright green at the point of disappearance.

As the sun sets, sunlight must shine through a much greater thickness of atmosphere than it does during most of the day. As the light travels from space (where there is no air) into and through the atmosphere, it is bent. Because of its longer wave-

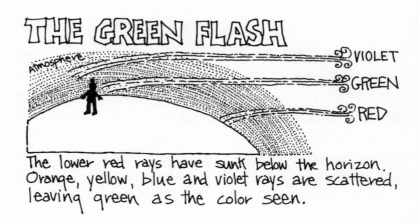

THE GREEN FLASH

Atmosphere

VIOLET
GREEN
RED

The lower red rays have sunk below the horizon. Orange, yellow, blue and violet rays are scattered, leaving green as the color seen.

length red is bent the least. Green is directly above red. The green flash occurs at that moment when the red has been cut off by the horizon. Red is removed and the violet and blue are largely scattered, so only green comes through. We see this, but only for a moment. If you don't see it the first time, don't give up. Keep trying and eventually you should be successful.

Satellite Viewing

Sometime while you are skywatching you may see a moving light that appears to be out among the stars. The light, which looks like a star, may move evenly from horizon to horizon, or it may disappear before it reaches the horizon. Sometimes the light may move a distance, disappear, and then reappear in a moment a bit farther along. This light is produced when sunlight is reflected from an artificial satellite, a space shuttle perhaps, or another large vehicle in an earth-circling orbit. There are several thousand objects in orbit, moving overhead every day. Many of them are bits and pieces of rocket engines and space probes, and a few of them are large enough to reflect enough sunlight to make them visible. It is not possible to give a satellite timetable. There are too many of them for newspapers to list them every day, but if you become a regular skywatcher there is a chance you will see a satellite, perhaps many of them.

Large numbers of space satellites are launched from Florida. Rockets push them toward the south and out over the Atlantic Ocean. A typical flight path is shown in the illustration.

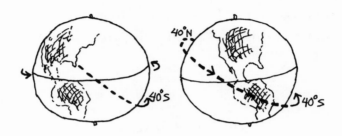

In this case the satellite will go southeast, reaching 40 degrees south of the equator. As it continues in its orbit it will reach 40 degrees north of the equator. During its flight, the earth turns under the path. Therefore the satellite passes over all parts of the earth that are located within these boundaries.

Most of the artifical objects in space are not visible. Even though they catch sunlight, the amount reflected to earth from them is too little to be picked up by unaided eyes. The objects remain in orbit because their speed is not changed. They are high enough so there are no air particles to cause friction that would slow their speed. If there were, gravitation would pull the object to earth. Even when this does happen, most people usually are not aware of it, for the object gets so hot that it vaporizes and never reaches the surface.

However, as a skywatcher you may see it happen. The satellite, or piece of debris, vaporizes because of the high temperature produced by friction with the earth's atmosphere, usually at an altitude of 60 miles or so above the surface. As the gases form, they glow because of the high temperature. The event appears to us as a meteor—a shooting star, as it is called.

In 1979, when Skylab came down, airplane pilots and people on the ground in Australia saw the light streaks. All of Skylab did not vaporize, however. Large pieces of it, some weighing up to several tons, fell to earth. A few of them fell over Australia, but fortunately most of them fell into the sea.

The SKYLAB is falling!

Skylab fell because it had been put into a low orbit. Also, engineers did not know that the sun would produce changes in our upper atmosphere. These changes caused the air to become more dense, and so to produce more friction.

When satellites are put high above earth they will stay in orbit for hundreds of years, or thousands, or in some cases forever. After all, the moon is in orbit around the earth and it has been there a long, long time—a few billions of years.

Someday you may see a light moving in the sky. At first it may look like a shooting star. But it goes much more slowly. If it persists, and if you see it move a considerable distance, you can be quite certain that you have seen a satellite or a space shuttle.

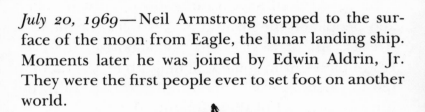

July 20, 1969—Neil Armstrong stepped to the surface of the moon from Eagle, the lunar landing ship. Moments later he was joined by Edwin Aldrin, Jr. They were the first people ever to set foot on another world.

AUGUST

The eighth month in our calendar has 31 days. In the old Roman calendar, this month was Sextilis, month number six. About 2000 years ago the Roman Emperor Augustus renamed the month to honor himself. The month was a very important one to him; it marked the time when he became ruler, it was the month in which he ended the civil wars that had ravaged the country, and it was the month when he defeated Egypt.

Meteor Showers

The middle of August is the best time of the year for seeing meteors. In other months you may see 6 or 8 in an hour, but around August 12 you may see as many as 50 an hour.

The August display is called the Perseid meteor shower. The meteors seem to move out and away from the constellation Perseus. The *id* at the end of the word comes from a Greek word meaning daughter of. These meteors were said to be the "daughters of Perseus," a mythical hero. Showers similar to the Perseids occur at other times of the year. In each case they are named after the constellation or star from which the meteors seem to radiate. The other principal meteor showers are listed in the table.

SHOWER	DATE OF GREATEST ACTIVITY	DAYS OF VISIBILITY	AVERAGE HOURLY RATE
Eta Aquarids (the star Eta in Aquarius)	MAY 5	18	20
Orionids	OCT. 21	8	20
Leonids	NOV. 16	4	15
Geminids	DEC. 13	6	50

Meteors can also be seen at other times, but not "showers" of them. Single displays are called sporadic meteors; they are unpredictable. For you to be able to see them or any other meteors the sky must be dark (no moon or city lights), and it must be clear of clouds. You must remain outside an hour or so, giving your eyes plenty of time to get used to the darkness.

80

A good way to watch for meteors is to join up with someone else. If there are two of you, lie down head to head so each person sees one half of the sky. It's even better if there are four people. Then each person watches only one quarter of the sky. If particles that cause meteors are evenly distributed in space, and moving randomly, the earth moves toward them in the hours after midnight and before dawn. The best time for meteor-watching is after midnight. Before midnight the night half of the earth is moving away from them.

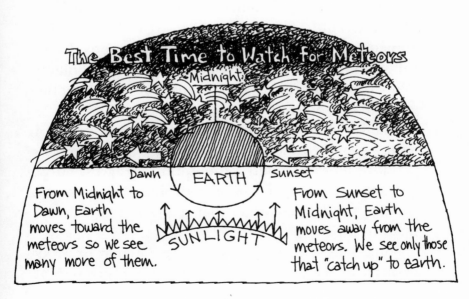

The Best Time to Watch for Meteors

Midnight

Dawn   EARTH   Sunset

From Midnight to Dawn, Earth moves toward the meteors so we see many more of them.

SUNLIGHT

From Sunset to Midnight, Earth moves away from the meteors. We see only those that "catch up" to earth.

A meteor looks like a streak of light, or a moving spot of light. When a meteor is especially bright it is called a fireball. If it is bright and there are pops and crackles, the meteor is called a bolide. Bolides are rare; most skywatchers never hear one, even though they watch the sky for years. (*Bolide* comes from a Greek word for missile.)

The light streak is produced by a meteoroid, a bit of solid material speeding through space. The meteoroids that produce showers seem to be debris left behind when a comet crossed Earth's orbit. When a meteoroid enters our atmosphere, friction causes it to become white hot. Also, the heat may cause the leading edge of the meteoroid to melt and change to gases. The high temperature causes atoms in the gases to lose electrons; they become ionized. As they regain electrons, the atoms release energy in the form of visible light. This light is the streak that we see. Sometimes the streak lasts for several seconds. Careful study of the light reveals that it often contains many colors. These colors are clues to identifying the gases that produce them.

Small meteoroids can produce a large amount of light. A meteoroid no larger than a walnut can produce a bright cloud a thousand feet across. Most meteors are produced by meteoroids that are much smaller, though, no larger than a grain of sand or the head of a pin.

Sometime while meteor-watching you may be lucky enough to see a streak that reaches the ground. It

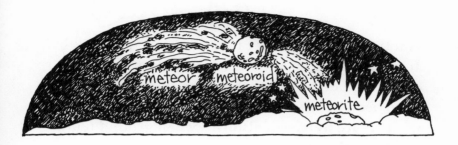

could be that the meteoroid really hit the ground. It would then be called a meteorite. If you could find the spot where it landed, you might find the meteorite there. But don't get your hopes up; finds like this are very rare. Large meteorites are even rarer; as size increases, so does scarcity.

Very few large meteorites have been found. Only ten weighing more than 9 metric tons are known; they were found in different parts of the world, in Mexico, Brazil, South Africa, and the United States. The largest one that is on display was found in Greenland. It is called Ahnighito. You can see it at the American Museum in New York City. Ahnighito weighs 30 945 kilograms (68,085 pounds).

In your skywatcher's journal you might want to record your meteor sightings. Put down the time and date, how long it seemed to last (one second, two seconds, or whatever), where you saw it, the constellation or segment of the sky where it appeared, whether it was a sporadic meteor or part of a shower. If there was a noticeable color, or brightness, put that down too.

Hail

Another sky event that often occurs in August is hail. It usually accompanies heavy thunderstorms, and so could happen any time there are such storms. There have been occasions when hail fell in winter. However, it is rare to have hailstorms when ground temperature is below freezing.

Hailstones (the name is used even though there are no stones in the ice balls) may be as large as golf balls or baseballs, or even larger. A hailstorm is frightening and dangerous. People can get under shelter, but crops that are exposed to hail may be ripped and cut to pieces. Hailstorms are disasters to farmers.

Air always contains water vapor. This is an odorless, colorless, and tasteless gas. And it is dry; there is no wetness in water vapor. When temperature drops, water vapor condenses. It changes to microscopic droplets. Clouds are collections of these water droplets.

On hot days of summer, air becomes very hot. It rises from the earth, and it is pushed up by colder air that digs under it. As the air rises, it cools; water vapor condenses into droplets and clouds form. The upward-moving air pushes the clouds higher and higher. They may tower to 10 or 12 kilometers. At the top of the cloud it is cold, and the droplets freeze into ice balls.

The ice then falls through the cloud. It passes through warmer air where moisture forms around the ice pellet. Upward-moving air again carries the pellet up with it. The water freezes, adding another layer to the ice pellet.

This may happen over and over again. If the upward-moving air is strong enough, and the cloud towers high enough, the pellet grows and grows. It may become very large before it becomes heavy enough to fall to earth. The largest reported hailstone fell in Kansas in 1970. It was 18.75 centimeters across (7½ inches) and weighed 800 grams (1.67 pounds). You can see why people get under a strong roof when there's a hailstorm.

Next time it hails where you are, collect a few ice pellets and put them in the freezer part of your refrigerator to keep them from melting. Take one at a time and slice it through the middle with a knife. If the hailstone is very small, hold it loosely with a pair of pliers. You'll probably see the separate layers of ice. Sometimes the layers are clear, but more often they are snowy white since air has been trapped in the ice.

August 1, 1818—Maria Mitchell, an American astronomer, was born at Nantucket, where there is now an observatory that bears her name. She discovered a comet, and made detailed studies of the sun and Jupiter.

The Autumn Stars

At 9:00 P.M. toward the middle of October look southward. About halfway between the horizon and overhead you'll see four stars that make a rather uneven rectangle. They are part of the constellation Pegasus, the Flying Horse. Actually, the upper star to the left (east) is in the constellation Andromeda. However, it is often considered one corner of the "square of Pegasus."

Look carefully for stars inside the square. Most people have been able to see only two or three. But there are observers who say they can see 32, and one observer said he could see 100. (He must have had telescopic eyes.)

Going eastward from Alpheratz, the star in the upper-left corner of Pegasus, there are three stars of about the same brightness. They are in Andromeda.

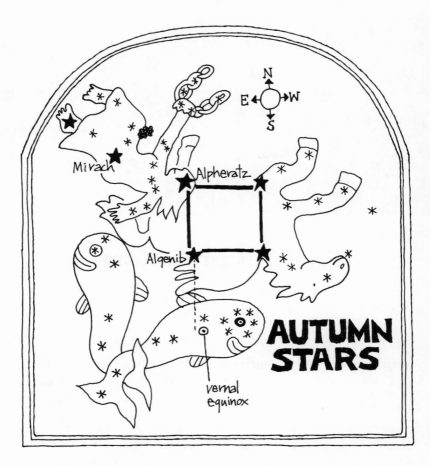

Mirach

Alpheratz

Algenib

AUTUMN
STARS

vernal
equinox

Just above Mirach, the middle star, and slightly to the
west is the great galaxy in Andromeda — a formation
that contains some 200 billion stars. It is located only
two million light years from us, making it a nearby
galaxy. Some people can see it with the unaided eye,
but most find that they need binoculars. Through
them, the galaxy appears as a fuzzy blotch of light.
Try to see it. When you do, keep in mind that you are

receiving ancient light, light that left the galaxy two million years ago.

Below the square of Pegasus is the head of one fish in the constellation Pisces, the Fishes. The fish extends eastward, and its tail entwines with another fish that swings in and up along the east side of the square.

If you take the distance between Alpheratz and Algenib and extend it southward below Algenib, you come to a point that is just slightly east of the vernal equinox. It is here that the ecliptic crosses the celestial equator. Spring begins when the sun is at this location.

In September all these stars are a bit east of south, and in November they are west of south.

SEPTEMBER

The ninth month of our calendar has 30 days. Its name comes from the Latin word *septem* ("seven") since in the early calendar it was the seventh month. Julius Caesar's calendar kept the name, although its place was then changed to number nine.

Anglo-Saxons called the month *gerst-monath* — the barley month. It was the time when barley was harvested. In Switzerland, September is still called *herbst-monath* — the month of harvests.

Fall Begins

Fall begins on or about September 23. It is the season when leaves fall from the trees. It is also called autumn; the word *autumn* comes from a Latin word which means maturity.

As in spring, the sun rises due east, and days and nights are once more equal the world over. And, as in spring, the sun is once more directly over the equator. In its path through the sky, the sun has reached the autumnal equinox. This is a point where the ecliptic (the sun's path) crosses the celestial equator. Presently it is located in the constellation Virgo. For the next six months the sun will be south of the celestial equator.

If you measure the elevation of the sun now as you did in spring, you will find that it is once again equal to 90 degrees minus our latitude.

Finding a North-South Line

You can use shadows and angles to determine an accurate north-south line. The shortest shadow cast by a stick, or a tree, is a north-south line. At solar noon, which during most of the year is not the same as noon by a clock, the sun is due south. Therefore, a stick casts a shadow due north.

In practice, it is often difficult to determine the shortest shadow. Another way to get a north-south line is as follows: fasten a stick upright to a block of wood; then place the block of wood on concrete, or blacktop, or on a large piece of cardboard, something on which you can draw lines.

Around ten in the morning put a mark at the tip of the shadow. Tie a string to a piece of chalk. Hold the string at the upright, and stretch the string to the mark. Using this radius as the distance, draw half a

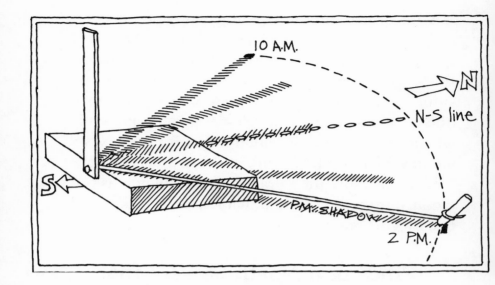

circle on the north side of the stick. Watch the shadow and you'll find that it will become shorter as noon approaches. After noon, the shadow will grow longer. Around two o'clock, it will reach the arc that you drew earlier. Mark that point. Draw lines from the two marks (the morning one and the afternoon one) to the upright to make a large angle.

Bisect the angle (divide it in two) and the line you produce will be a north-south line. Bisect the angle as follows: hold the string at the A.M. point and strike an arc toward the P.M. point and on the side away from the upright — the north side. Do the same operation using the P.M. point. The two arcs intersect. Draw a line from that intersection to the upright. This is the north-south line.

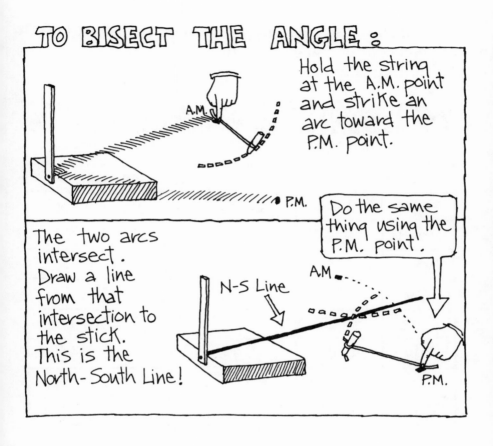

Harvest Moon and Hunters' Moon

If you keep track of the times that the full moon rises, you will find that it rises later each night, and that the delay in moonrise from one night to the next changes during the year. Each night the moon rises about one hour later. Sometimes the delay is more than an hour; at other times of the year it is much less. An

93

almanac lists the times of moonrise. Check the intervals of rising of the full moon during the year, and you'll find figures something like these:

| MOON RISE at 40° NORTH LATITUDE | | | | |
MONTH	Day Before Full	Full	Day After Full	Delays (minutes)
Jan.	4:17	5:13	6:12	56, 59
Feb.	5:01	6:05	7:10	64, 65
March	4:53	6:00	7:08	57, 68
April	5:56	7:07	8:19	71, 72
May	5:53	7:06	8:17	73, 71
June	5:52	7:02	8:07	70, 65
July	6:48	7:43	8:31	55, 48
Aug.	5:38	6:16	6:50	38, 34
Sept.	5:22	5:54	6:27	32, 33 *
Oct.	4:27	5:00	5:35	33, 35 X
Nov.	4:11	4:50	5:32	39, 40
Dec.	4:15	5:04	5:56	49, 52

* Harvest Moon
X Hunter's Moon

The delay in moonrise from one night to the next occurs because the moon moves around the earth. In one month (about 30 days) the moon goes around

94

once; it goes full circle, or through 360 degrees. Therefore, each day it goes through about 12 degrees (30 × 12 = 360). Earth must turn a bit more than once to "catch up" with the moon. The time required for earth to catch up to the moon, to see it once more on the horizon, is the delay (or retardation) in moonrise.

The moon's path through the sky is along the ecliptic (the path of the sun) or nearly so. The angle that the ecliptic makes with the horizon changes through the year. It is greatest in spring, and least in autumn.

In the spring the moon moves 12 degrees along the ecliptic. In fall, it also moves 12 degrees along the ecliptic. In spring it takes 24 hours plus an hour or more for the horizon to move to the new location of the moon. In the fall, it takes 24 hours plus only 32 or 33 minutes for the horizon to move to the moon's new position.

This full moon occurs around September 23, the time of the autumnal equinox. As in the case of all full moons, it is opposite the sun. That means the full moon rises in the east as the sun sets in the west. In autumn the full moon rises early for several nights, lighting up the evening sky. Autumn is the harvest season. This particular moon was called the harvest moon because it provided light by which farmers could work late into the evening to bring in the harvest.

In October the moon also provides a continuation

of daylight into evenings. It was called the hunters'
moon because it gave light for hunters of ancient days
to hunt down game.

Hurricanes

During summer the southern seas have warmed —
the Gulf of Mexico, the Caribbean Sea, and the
Atlantic Ocean southeast of Florida. These are the
places where hurricanes begin, usually in August and
September. The skies may be bright and clear a day
or two before a hurricane reaches you, so skywatching gives you no clue. You must listen to the weather
reports to know what is developing.

A hurricane is a violent tropical storm. Hurricane
winds blow at least 119 kilometers (74 miles) an hour.
And they have sometimes reached 322 kilometers
(200 miles) an hour.

The storm begins over the southern seas. In
satellite photos it first appears as a dark, swirling
doughnut of clouds. Weather watchers study these
pictures to see how the storm will develop. It may
grow very large, often reaching a diameter of 483
kilometers (300 miles). At the center of the hurricane,
called the eye, air pressure is low. The air around the
eye rushes into the low pressure region. As the air
rushes in, it curves. The hurricane is a huge mass of
air speeding around and into the eye.

Prevailing winds push the eye of the hurricane and the air around it. Often the winds carry the hurricane to coastal regions. In 1969 sections of the coast of Mississippi were knocked flat by hurricane Camille. (Hurricanes are named in alphabetical order; the first of the season may begin with A — Alice, for example, the second with B — Bert. Camille was the third storm of 1969.)

The screaming wind bends trees over. Some are pulled out of the ground and laid flat. Even brick buildings are blown apart. Mobile homes are picked up, even when they are tied down. Heavy seas pick up boats and drop them in streets. Cars are overturned. The entire coast may be under several feet of raging water. People are caught up and carried away.

Fortunately, hurricanes do not come as surprises. Weather people watch the storms develop and issue warnings about them.

Someone has said that the force of a hurricane is like 40 atom bombs going off each second. No one can stop a hurricane. But people need not be killed by them if they get away from the coastal areas.

Today more people live near the coast than ever before, and many of them have never seen a hurricane. They may not pay attention to the warnings. But they should. Once a hurricane hits, the wind blows hard enough to knock people over; the ocean washes over the coast, roads are flooded. It is too late for people to go inland.

If a hurricane comes close, people are warned to

leave their houses and go inland. If they must stay at home, they should remember:

Electric power will probably go off, so they should have a flashlight, candles, and dry matches.

Water pipes may be broken, so water should be stored in a clean bathtub.

They must stay indoors; outdoors they could be knocked over, or hit by a falling tree.

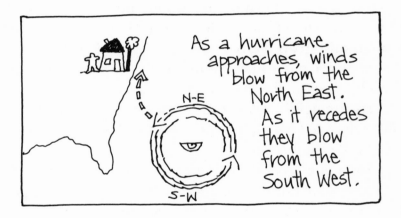

As a hurricane approaches, winds blow from the North East. As it recedes they blow from the South West.

Often people in a hurricane are fooled when the wind stops suddenly, and the skies clear. They think the storm is over. But it isn't; they are in the eye of the hurricane. When the storm approaches, the wind blows from the northeast, and it may blow for several hours. The storm center moves along, and when the eye reaches you the wind stops, but the storm keeps moving. In an hour or so, often less, the winds blow

WIND SPEED (m.p.h.)	Sir Francis Beaufort's WIND SCALE
0	Smoke rises up
1-3	Smoke drifts
4-7	Leaves rustle; Flags stir
8-12	Leaves and twigs move
13-18	Branches move; Flags flap
19-24	Small trees sway; Flags ripple
25-31	Large branches move; Flags beat
32-38	Whole trees move; Flags extend
39-46	Twigs break; walking is difficult
47-54	Signs, antennas blow down
55-73	Trees uprooted- Damage to Buildings
74 and more..... Hurricanes	Countryside devastated

TROPICAL STORMS

again, just as hard as before. But now they blow from the southwest.

Hurricanes are killer storms. But no one need be killed by them. Listen for hurricane warnings. Know what to do, and do it.

At the beginning of the nineteenth century, Sir Francis Beaufort, an admiral in the British navy, devised a scale for measuring the wind's force, which the U.S. Weather Service has adapted for use today. By watching objects that are moved by the wind, you can get a good idea of how fast the wind is blowing.

September 10, 1892—Arthur Compton, American physicist, was born. He discovered a great deal about cosmic rays, the subatomic particles that abound in outer space.

September 18, 1819—Jean Bernard Leon Foucault, French scientist and inventor, was born. He invented the Foucault pendulum, which proved that the earth was rotating.

OCTOBER

Our tenth month, of 31 days, was month number eight (*Octobris*) to the early Romans. It became month number ten in the Julian calendar. For short periods the month carried the name of other Roman emperors — Germanicus, Antoninus, and Herculeus — but they did not last. At one time it was named Faustinus in honor of Faustina, wife of Antoninus. But that name was never accepted either.

The Slavs call it the yellow month because of the turning of the leaves. Anglo-Saxons called it *winterfylleth*. The full moon ("fylleth") of this month was supposed to signal the start of winter.

Visitors from Space

Sometime when you are skywatching, you may see something you won't be able to explain. To you, it will be a UFO — an Unidentified Flying Object. If you see a UFO, remain calm. Not all people do. In fact, back in 1938, people were far from calm; they were frantic. And they hadn't even seen a UFO; they only heard about it on the radio.

On October 30, 1938, Orson Welles and the Mercury Theater Company broadcast a radio version of a book called *The War of the Worlds*. This is an exciting story by H. G. Wells which tells of the invasion of the earth by Martians. The broadcast was intended to be a Halloween prank, but it was presented as though it were a news program coming from southern New Jersey. It was very realistic. "Newscasters" told of strange ships descending to earth and of creatures getting out of them and destroying people and animals.

When people heard the program, many thought it was a real news broadcast. Some put their possessions in their cars and sped away from New Jersey. The "Martians" were spreading across the countryside and people were frantic to get as far away as possible. You couldn't blame them, because this was just before the start of World War II and the idea of an invasion seemed reasonable, especially to people along the east coast. Your library may have a recording of the broadcast. If you can do so, listen to it and think how you might have felt if you believed it was a real news program.

People believe what they want to believe.

That seems to be true, no matter what the evidence may be. Since that time, and long before, there have been many people who believe that they have seen spaceships which must have come from other worlds. Not only that, some people say they have seen the ships land, and creatures coming out of them. There are even people who say they have been captured by the creatures, taken aboard the ships, and carried into space. One person said she was taken to Venus, where she met its ruler. After a while, she said, the ship brought her back to the earth.

The idea of visitors from other worlds is fascinating, and writers have used the theme in exciting stories. But the possibility of visitors actually landing on Earth, or even surveying us from orbit, is very slim. So, when you're skywatching, try to find a reasonable explanation for everything you see.

A light moving across the sky may be an artificial satellite or sunlight reflecting from a weather balloon. Some strange lights have turned out to be sunlight reflected from gases released at high altitudes. Weathermen track these gases to discover the patterns of air movement. And there are other explanations of UFOs. The planet Venus often appears to be moving across the sky; light from advertising signs is sometimes reflected from low-hanging clouds.

Very likely you'll find that what first appears to be a UFO will eventually become identified — it will be an IFO. Then again, who knows, maybe some night you'll actually see something that no one can explain.

Guide to Planet Watching

The crisp, cool nights of October are good for planet-watching. However, planets can also be seen among the stars at other times. As you become familiar with stars and constellations, the planets will become more and more obvious; they look like stars. But you know they are not because they don't belong to the constellations where they appear.

When the planets are visible they will be in one of the constellations of the zodiac. This is a belt around the sky made of twelve adjoining constellations. We have already discussed many of them. The twelve constellations are Pisces, Aquarius, Capricornus, Sagittarius, Scorpius, Libra, Virgo, Leo, Cancer, Gemini, Taurus, and Aries. These are the constellations that lie along the ecliptic, the path that the sun appears to follow in the course of one year. And, since the planets are related to the sun, this is the path along which the planets are to be seen.

Mercury, Venus, Mars, Jupiter, and Saturn are the five planets that can be seen with the unaided eye. Mercury is close to the sun, so it always appears either at sunrise or sunset. Since it is in the twilight sky, Mercury never appears very bright; there is not enough contrast.

Venus can be very bright. When it is the "morning star" it can be seen in the east up to a few hours before sunrise. At other times it is the "evening star," appearing up to a few hours after sunset. It can never be seen around midnight, since it is located between the earth and the sun.

At times Mars, Jupiter, and Saturn may be seen throughout the night. An almanac gives their rising and setting times. Often newspapers carry the same information, and they sometimes tell the constellation in which the planet can be found.

All of the planets move among the stars. Those that have the longest periods move most slowly. Mars moves fast enough for you to see changes over a period of a few days. Once you have located the planet, you may find it interesting to map its motions. Make a sketch of the sky, showing the planet and its relation to nearby stars. A few evenings later, compare your sketch with the sky. Place another dot in your sketch to show the new position of Mars. Continue doing this for several weeks or months. You may be surprised to see that the planet appears to stop, move backward, and then resume its original motion. Astronomers say that it *retrogrades*.

This motion caused consternation among ancient observers. To explain it, they said the planet moved on a circle, the center of which moved around the earth. The idea was accepted for thousands of years. Today we can explain the motion in other ways. Both Earth and Mars go around the sun. We move faster than Mars so we catch up and pass Mars. As we do, the planet appears to move backwards. In the same way, when a moving train passes another moving train, the one that is passed seems to be going backwards.

Practice planet-watching. Locate planets by referring to an almanac or your newspaper. It doesn't take long to become familiar with the planets. They will become very apparent as you learn the constellations and the stars that are in them.

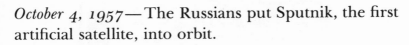

October 4, 1957—The Russians put Sputnik, the first artificial satellite, into orbit.

October 14, 1947—Charles E. Yeager was the first person to fly a plane faster than the speed of sound.

NOVEMBER

November comes from the Latin *novem* ("nine"). Before the Julian Calendar November was the ninth month. It is now number eleven and it has 30 days. The Roman senate wanted to call it Tiberius to honor their ruler, but he declined the offer.

Anglo-Saxons called the month *wind-monath;* it is still the time for windstorms in that part of the world. They also called it *blod-monath* ("blood month"), perhaps because on occasion the moon seemed to have a reddish color.

William Herschel and the Shape of the Galaxy

All the stars appear to be the same distance from us. If you've never noticed this, think of distance the next time you look at the stars. There is no way you can tell from its appearance whether a star is near or far. The stars appear to be placed on a sphere that surrounds the earth—the celestial sphere, as it is called. For thousands of years people believed that this was truly the case—the center of the universe was the earth; the sun, moon, and planets went around the earth; all were contained inside a hollow ball; the surface of the ball was studded with stars.

This idea persisted into the eighteenth century. If there was a single pioneer of a new and different model of the universe, it was Sir William Herschel, who was born in Germany on November 15, 1738. As a young man he left Germany and went to England, where he lived for the rest of his life.

Herschel was an accomplished musician and also a maker of scientific instruments. He sold many of the telescopes he made. But he also used them himself to study the sky.

Herschel had a startling idea: all the stars are not the same distance from us. He believed that all the stars are equally bright. Today we know they are not, but Herschel assumed that they were. Differences in brightness are only apparent, he said. A light that is close to you is brighter than the same light at a distance. And so it is with the stars, he said. Bright stars are close to us, and dim stars are not. The dimmer a star, the farther away it is.

Night after night, Herschel studied the stars. If you do as he did, you'll discover, as Herschel did, that some regions of the sky have many bright stars, while other regions have few, if any. Herschel plotted the positions and brightness and so was able to make a drawing that revealed the position of the stars that "surrounded" us. Unlike the old "celestial sphere," Herschel's diagram was irregular. Where there were dim stars the formation had long arms. Herschel's drawing was one of the earliest models of our galaxy — the star formation of which we are part. (At the time Herschel made his drawing, people believed he was representing the entire universe.) Herschel's model of the galaxy was flat, not round. Herschel believed this because he saw many more stars along the Milky Way region than at locations 90 degrees from the Milky Way. You can see this for yourself. Stars become less densely packed as we look into regions away from the Milky Way.

Much later, in the 1920s, it was found that our galaxy is only one of billions of other galaxies in the universe. Also, astronomers found that our galaxy is disc-shaped, and we are not at the center, as almost everyone believed, but some 30,000 light years away from it.

When you look at the sky you have no way of knowing these things. The galaxy seems to be just what people said it was thousands of years ago: a great turning ball on the inside of which the stars are fastened.

Keeping Weather Records

On November 1, 1870, weather service was begun in the United States. Keeping records of weather — rainfall, snowfall, clouds, and storms — started at that time. At first, information came from only a few scattered stations, and the data were not sufficient to make reliable forecasts. Today there are weather stations all over the country. Information is gathered from them and from ships at sea. And, most important, weather satellites gather pictures of worldwide cloud formations and weather systems.

Weather is a favorite topic of conversation because our lives are regulated by the weather. In fact, our lives are sometimes completely dependent upon it. Usually we are not conscious of the connection between lifestyle and weather. But we certainly are during periods of heavy rain that causes flooding, or of droughts that cause crops to dry up, or when there are storms that cause widespread destruction.

As a skywatcher you should find it interesting to become familiar with various types of clouds, and to learn how they are related to weather in your area. You'll find that you can make forecasts that are quite reliable — often just as reliable as those made by professional weather forecasters. Your forecast will be for your own local area, which is much easier than forecasting the weather for a large region.

Weathermen have found that the most important

factors in predicting weather are the kinds of clouds in the sky, the amount of clouds, and the wind direction. The main kinds of clouds and the weather that in most locations is associated with them are shown below:

Your records may show that the various kinds of clouds indicate different weather in your area. This is entirely likely, because local conditions, such as a high

Cloud Cover	CIRRUS				ALTOCUMULUS				ALTOSTRATUS			
Wind Direction	N	E	S	W	N	E	S	W	N	E	S	W
WEATHER	FAIR AND COOL	FAIR AND COOL	WARMER (SHOWERS?)	FAIR	LITTLE CHANGE	LITTLE CHANGE	SHOWERS	FAIR	FAIR AND COOL	CLOUDY	BECOMING FAIR	SHOWERS

mountain, nearness to the sea, or a broad plain, may have a strong effect on local weather.

Wind direction determines how the clouds move, and so it affects weather. Flags fly with the wind and are good indicators of where the wind is blowing from. A south wind blows from the south toward the north; an east wind blows from east to west, and so on.

NIMBUS				CUMULUS				STRATOCUMULUS			
N	E	S	W	N	E	S	W	N	E	S	W
BECOMING FAIR	STORMY, THEN FAIR	BECOMING FAIR	STORMY, THEN FAIR	SHOWERY, COOL	SHOWERY	SHOWERS, THEN FAIR	FAIR	UNSETTLED	LITTLE CHANGE	SHOWERS	LITTLE CHANGE

If there are no direction indicators such as flags, you can make a pointer. Get a piece of wood 30 or 40 centimeters long. (A dowel about 1 centimeter in diameter is the best.) Put the dowel in a vise and make a saw-cut 3 or 4 centimeters deep in one end. Use a light saw that has teeth close together. Cut a tailpiece

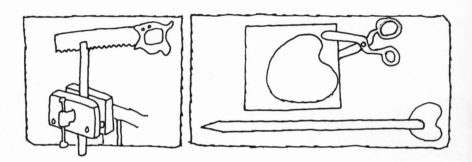

out of cardboard to fit into the saw-cut. It would be better to use a piece of plastic, which would be waterproof. If the saw-cut is a little large you may have to set the tailpiece with glue. You can whittle a point at the other end of the dowel.

When the pointer is finished, move it back and forth on the edge of a ruler until the pointer balances. Mark the location with a pencil. Drill a small hole at the balance point of the dowel. Be sure the hole lines up with the tailpiece. The hole should be a bit more than halfway through the dowel. Push a small piece of heavy aluminum foil into the hole so it lines the bottom of it.

aluminum foil in hole

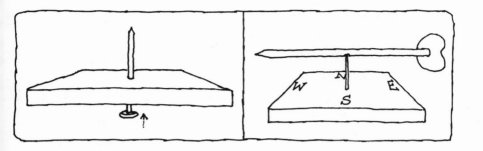

Use a board 20 or 30 centimeters square for the base of the pointer. Drive a long, thin nail through the center of the board so the point of the nail is straight up. (Hammer carefully to be sure the nail is straight.) The pointer will pivot on the point of the nail. Put the base on top of a fence post or tree stump. Or you might put it on a stone wall. Try to place it where it will be in the wind. Before you fasten down the base, put an N (for north) on it. Line up the N with north and then nail the base in place or weight it down with a stone. (You can find north with a compass; or the day's shortest shadow will be a north-south line.)

The pointer will point *into* the wind; if the wind is from the east, the pointer will point east.

Now you are ready to skywatch for clouds and wind directions. On a calendar or in your journal put down the kind of clouds. If a quarter or less of the sky is covered, the sky is considered to be clear. Also, record the direction of the wind. Try to do this always at the same times of day. Suppose you do it first at eight in the morning. Around five o'clock in the evening of the same day put down the weather at that time — cloudy, rainy, clearing, or whatever. Gradually you will build your own chart of clouds, wind direction, and weather.

Keep your record for several weeks or months if possible. After a while, you may see a pattern. For example, you may find that in the summer, when there are altocumulus clouds, the weather becomes fair if the wind is from the west; if the wind is from the south or east there may be showers later on. After a while your observations of the wind and the clouds will enable you to make forecasts for later in the day. Very likely, the longer you keep records, the more accurate your forecasts will become. Maybe you will become the weather prophet of your neighborhood.

November 20, 1883 — The United States went on Standard Time. Before that, each town and hamlet had a different time. When you traveled, even only a few miles, you had to keep changing your clock.

BIBLIOGRAPHY

Adler, Irving and Ruth Adler. *The Calendar.* New York: John Day, 1967.

Branley, Franklyn M. *A Book of Flying Saucers for You.* New York: Thomas Y. Crowell, 1973.

――――. *Color: From Rainbows to Lasers.* New York: Thomas Y. Crowell, 1977.

――――. *Columbia and Beyond: The Story of the Space Shuttle.* New York: Collins, 1979.

――――. *The Moon: Jack and Jill and Other Legends.* Lexington, Mass.: Ginn, 1972.

Brown, Hanbury. *Man and the Stars.* New York: Oxford, 1979.

Cohen, Daniel. *What's Happening to Our Weather?* New York: M. Evans, 1979.

Galt, Tom. *Seven Days from Sunday.* New York: Thomas Y. Crowell, 1956.

Holmes, Edward. *Great Men of Science.* New York: Warwick Press, 1979.

Knight, David C. *UFO's: A Pictorial History.* New York: McGraw Hill, 1979.

Laycock, George. *Tornadoes: Killer Storms.* New York: McKay, 1979.

Rey, H. A. *Find the Constellations.* Boston: Houghton Mifflin, 1976.

――――. *The Stars: A New Way to See Them.* Boston: Houghton Mifflin, 1952.